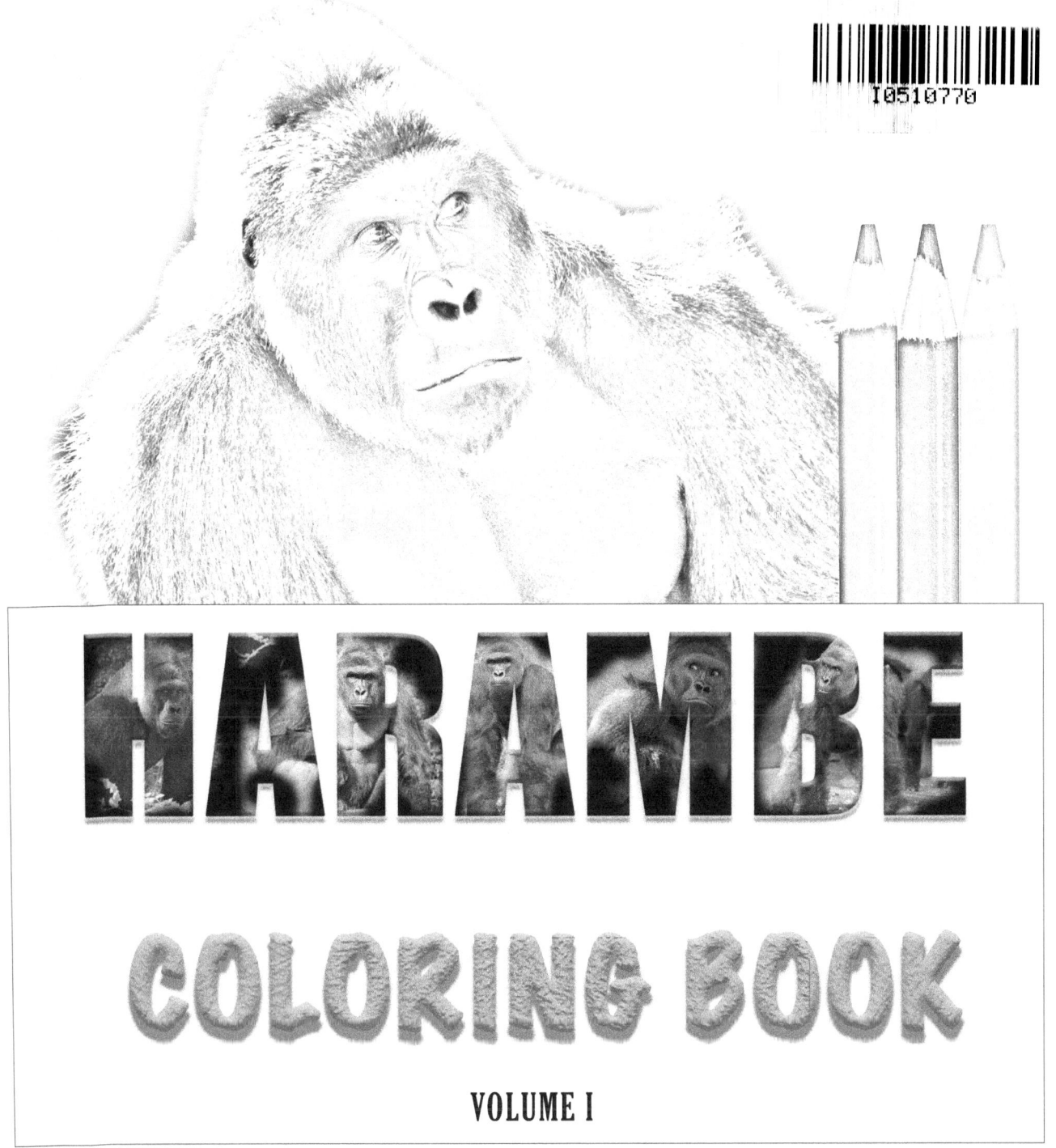

HARAMBE

COLORING BOOK

VOLUME I

Front cover and inside pages designed by Donald Owen, Creative Dynamics Multimedia Publishing.

I0510770

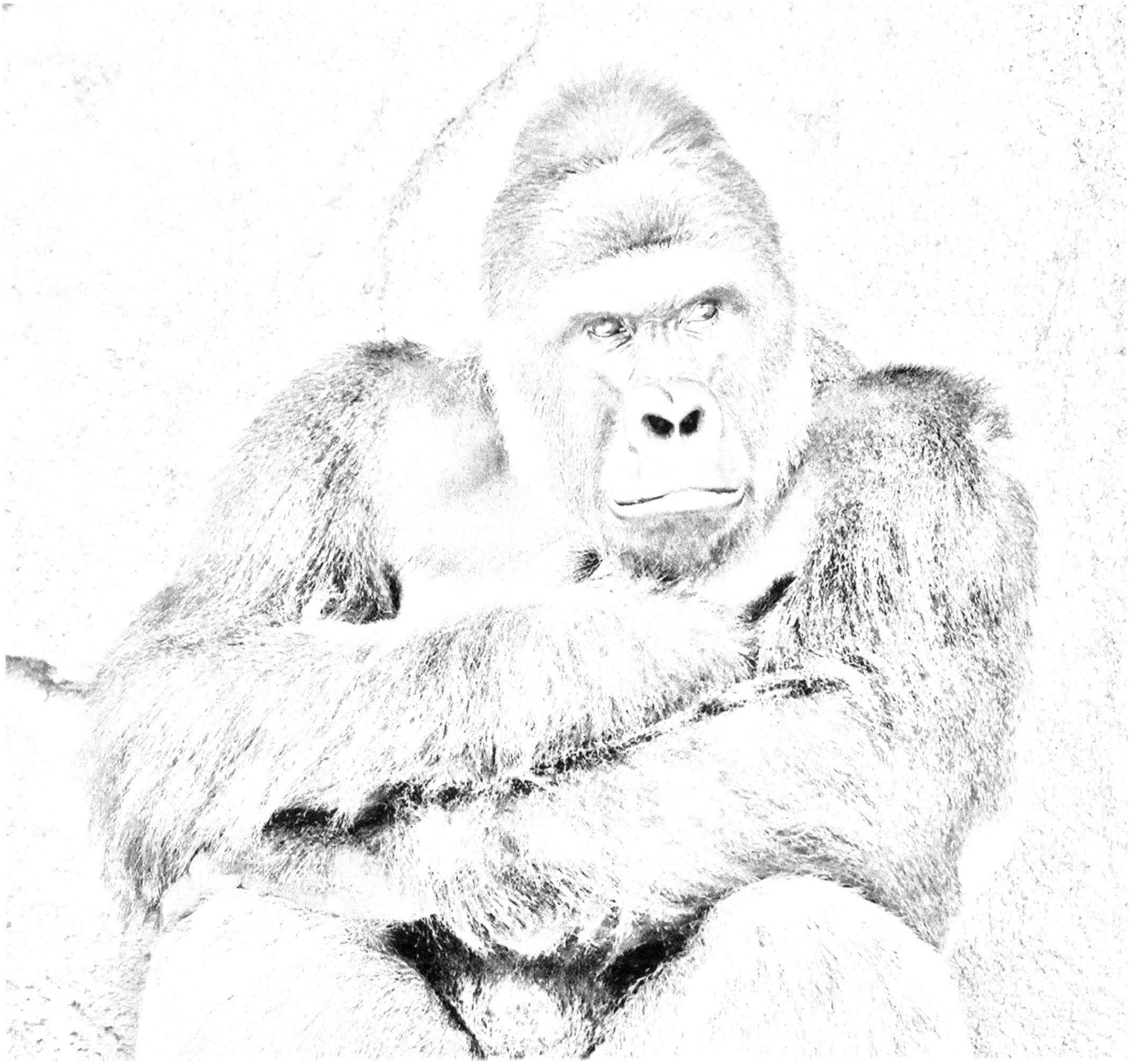

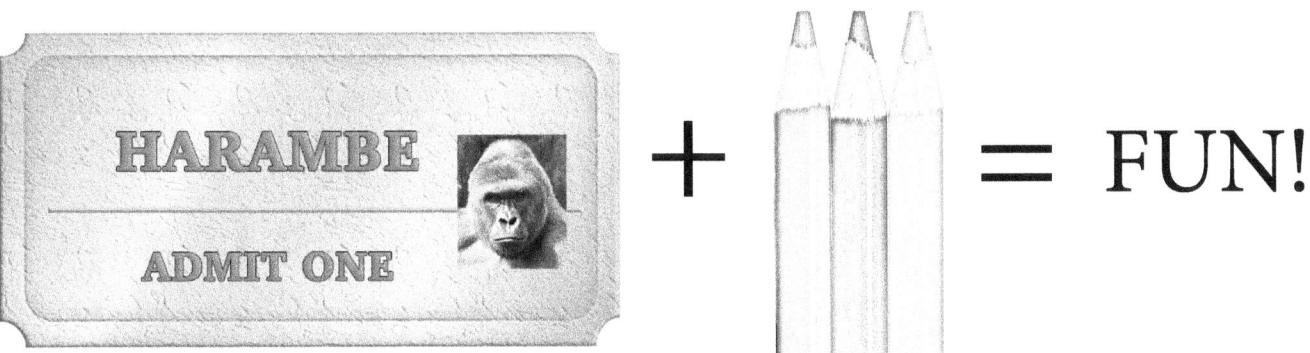

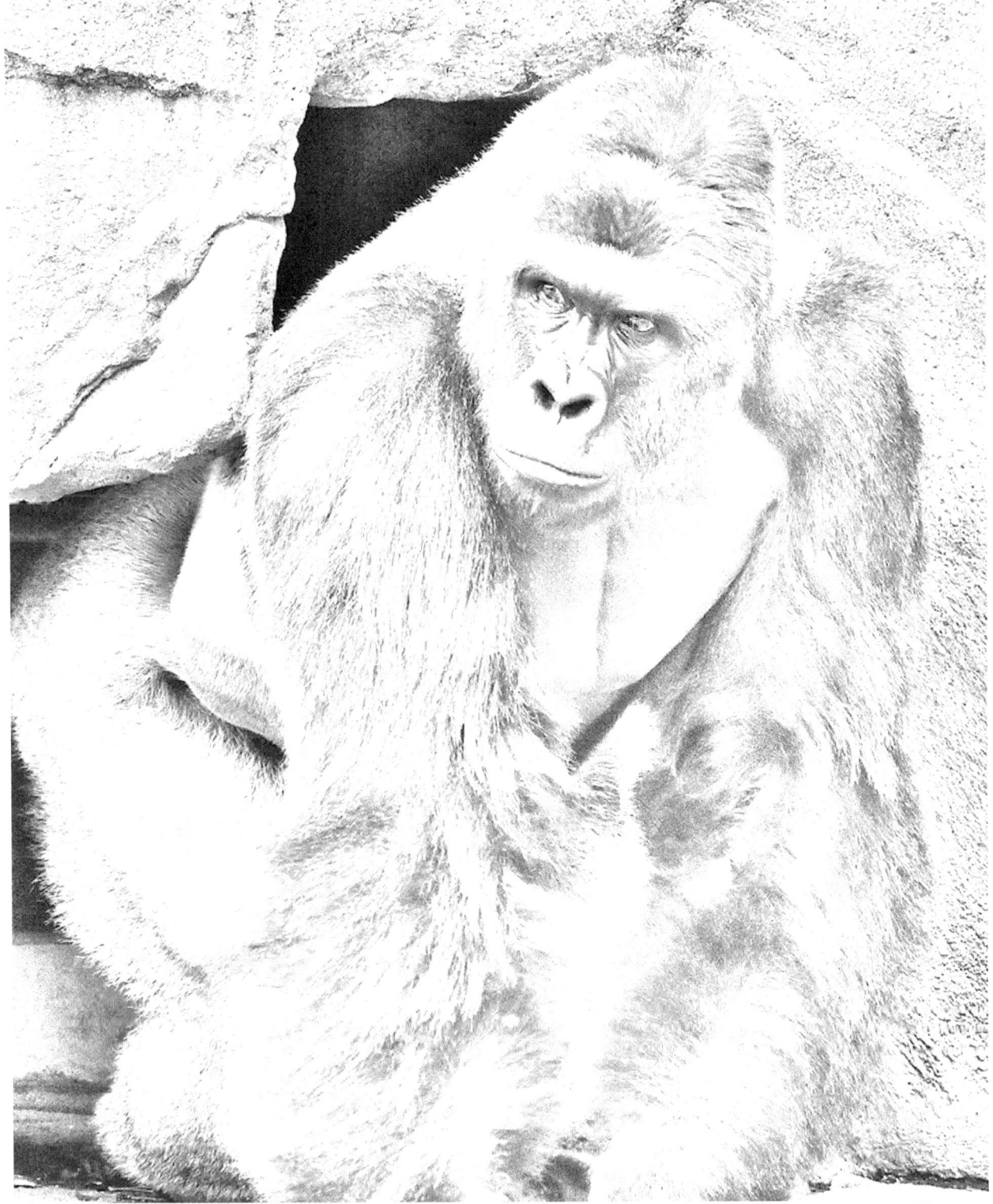

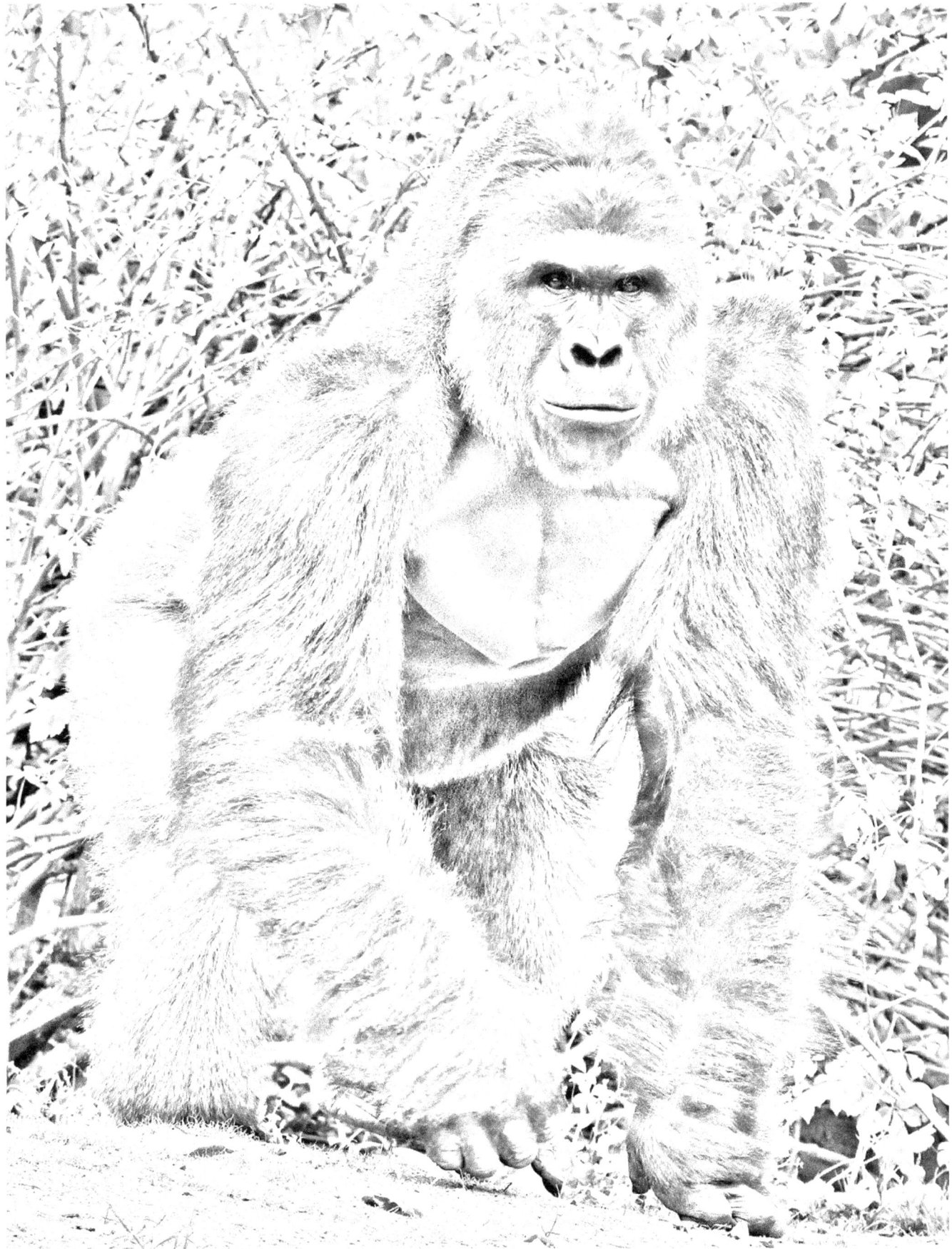

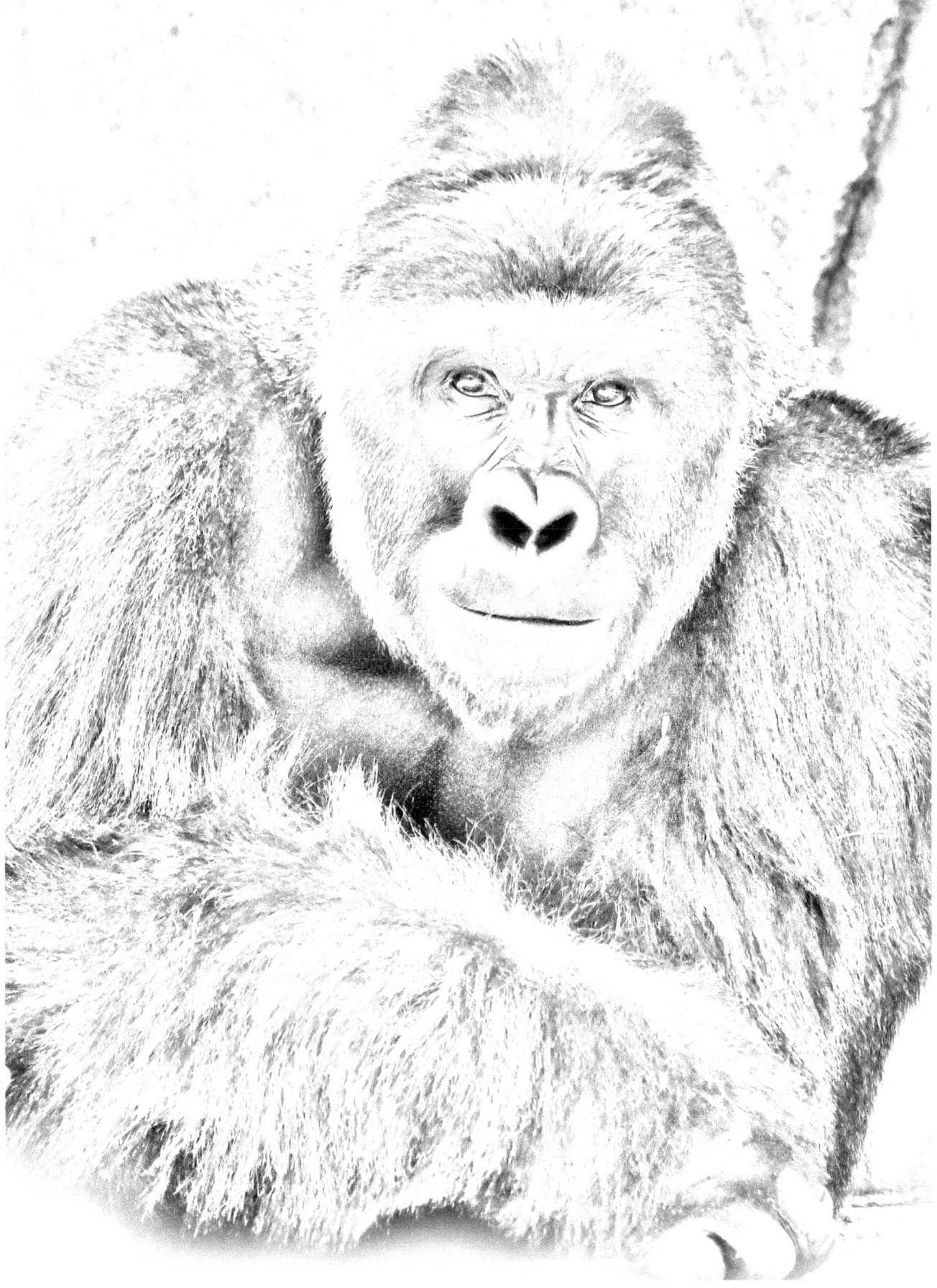

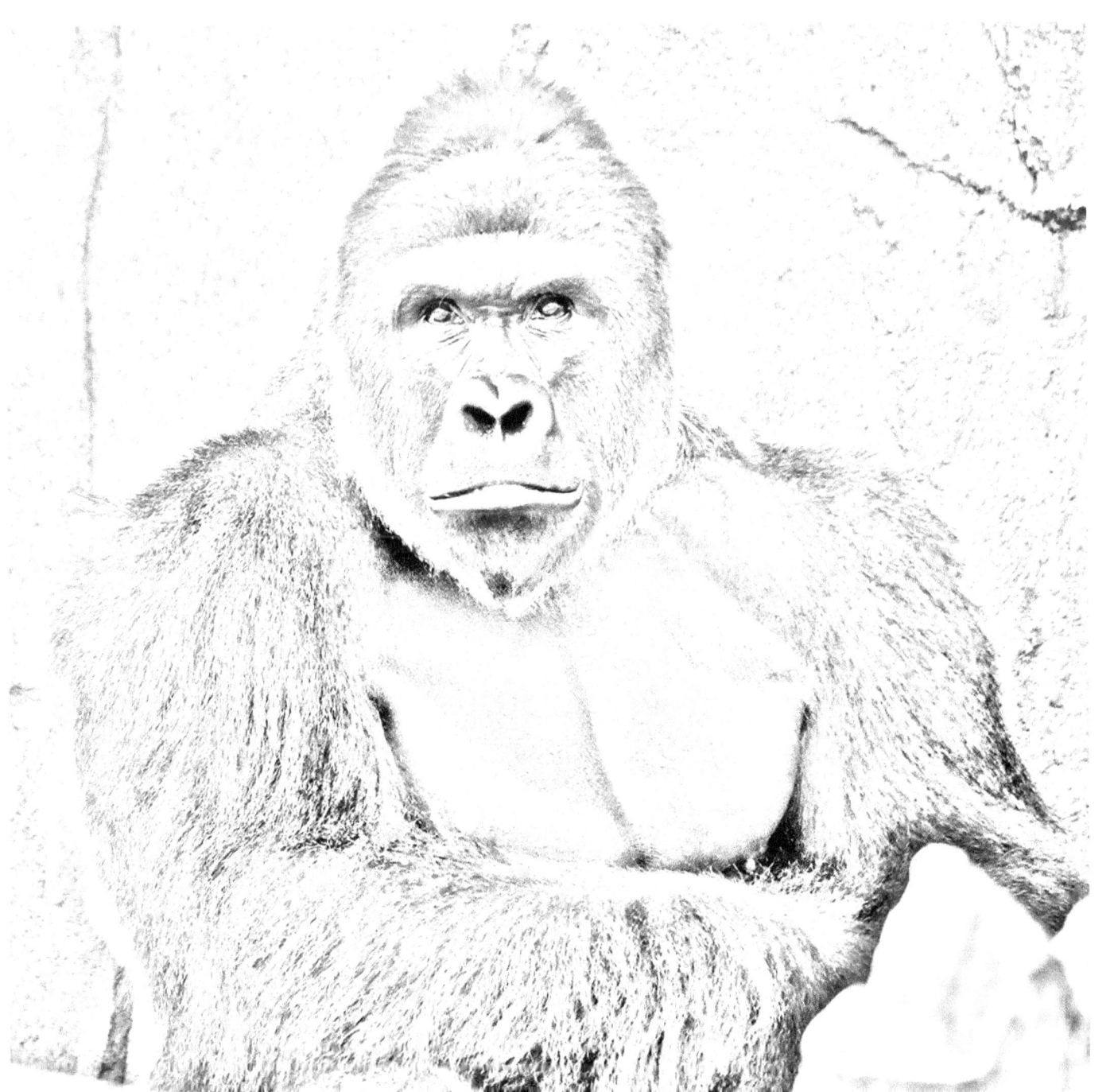

HARAMBE

WESTERN LOWLAND
SILVERBACK GORILLA

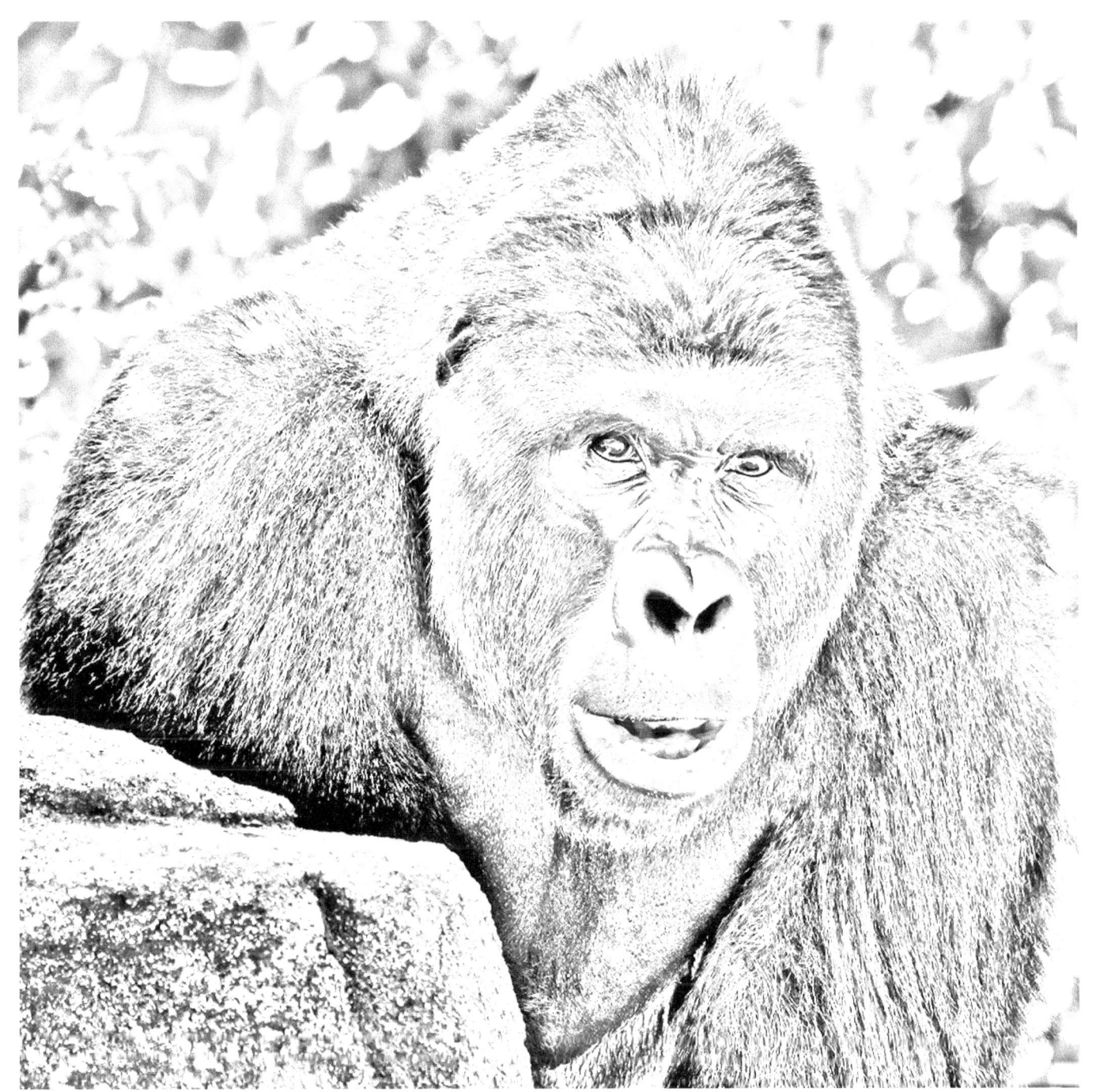

HARAMBE

NATURAL HABITAT IS IN WESTERN AFRICA

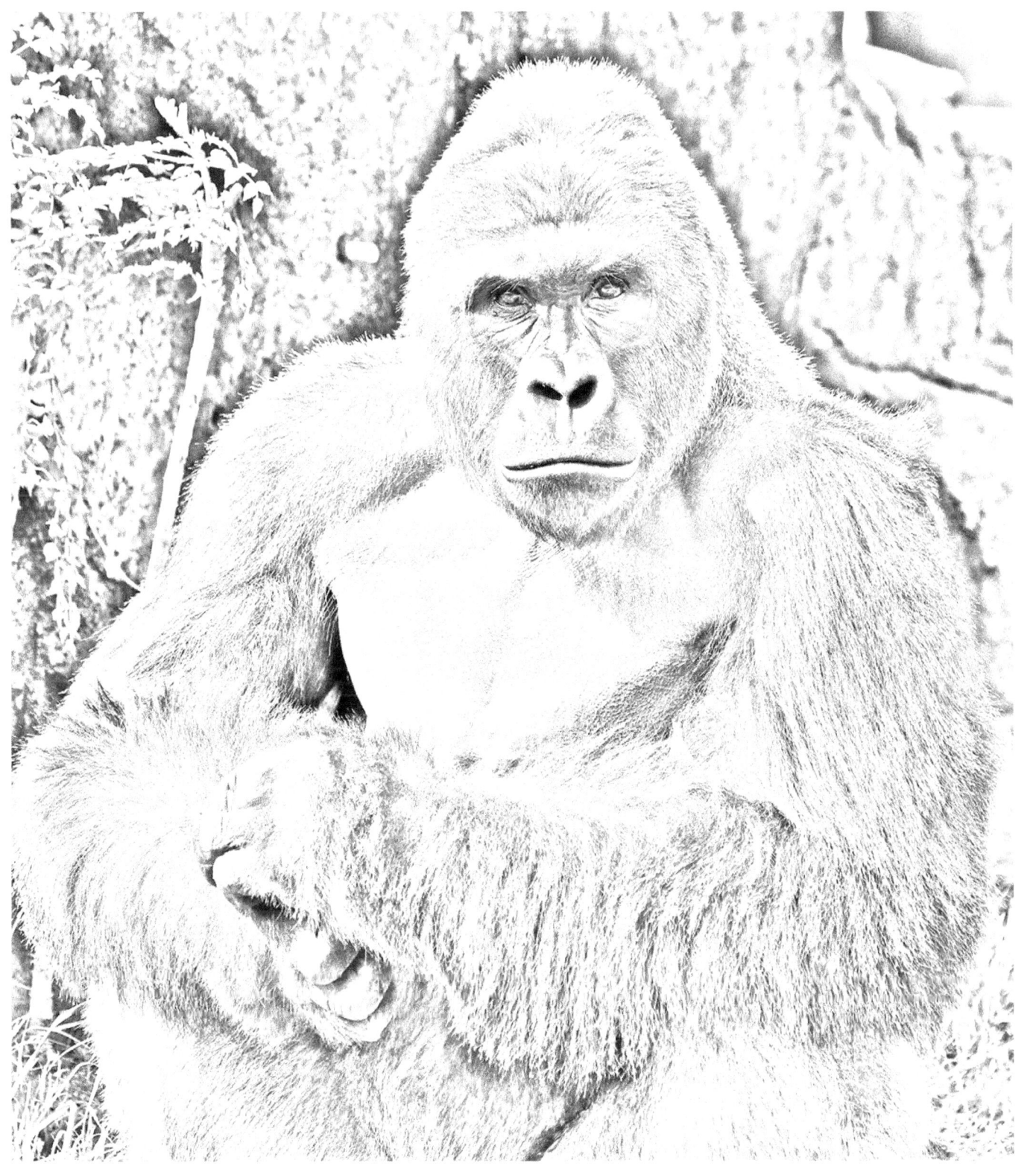

THE KING OF CINCINNATI

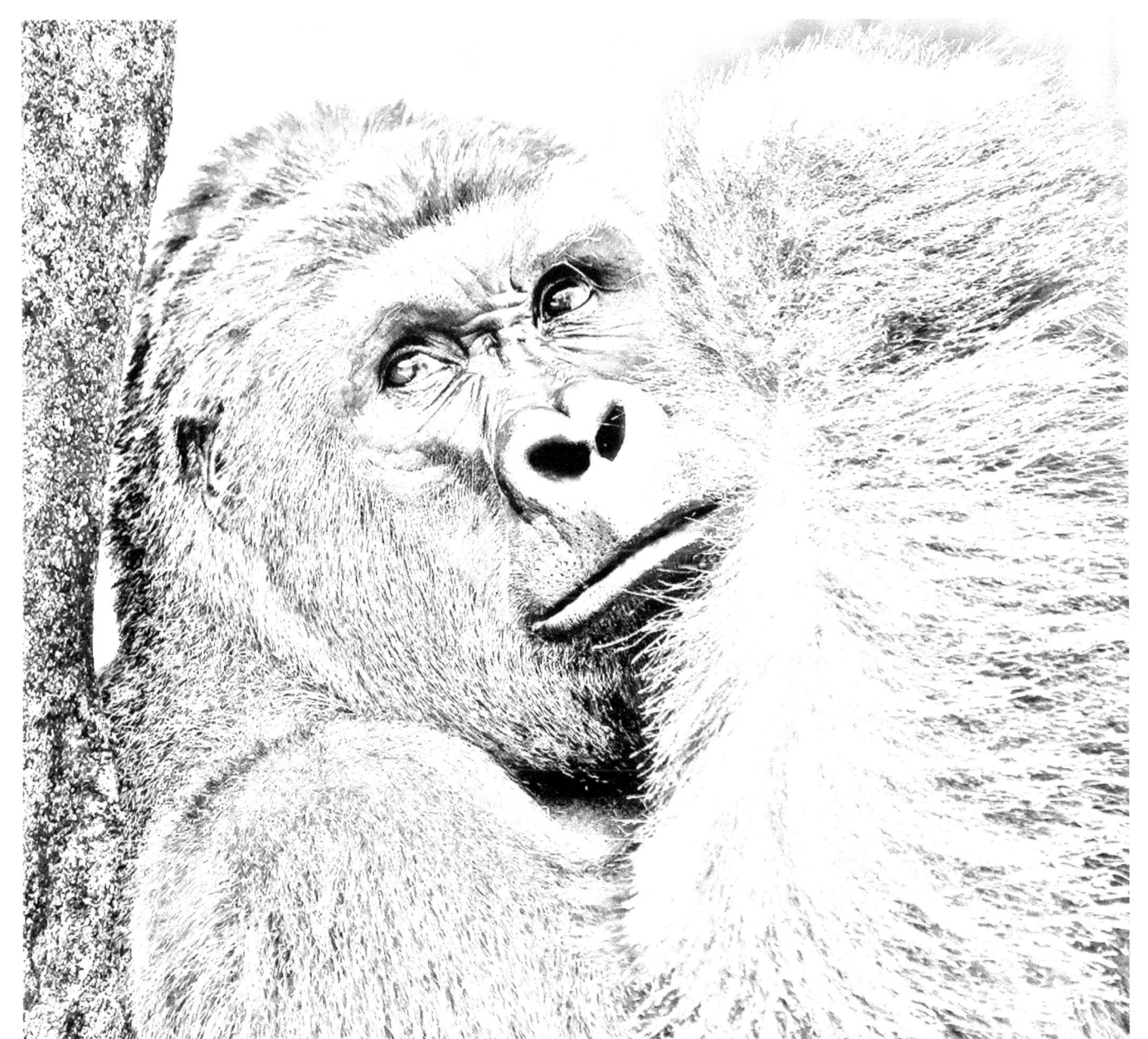

HARAMBE

POPULAR ATTRACTION AT THE CINCINNATI ZOO

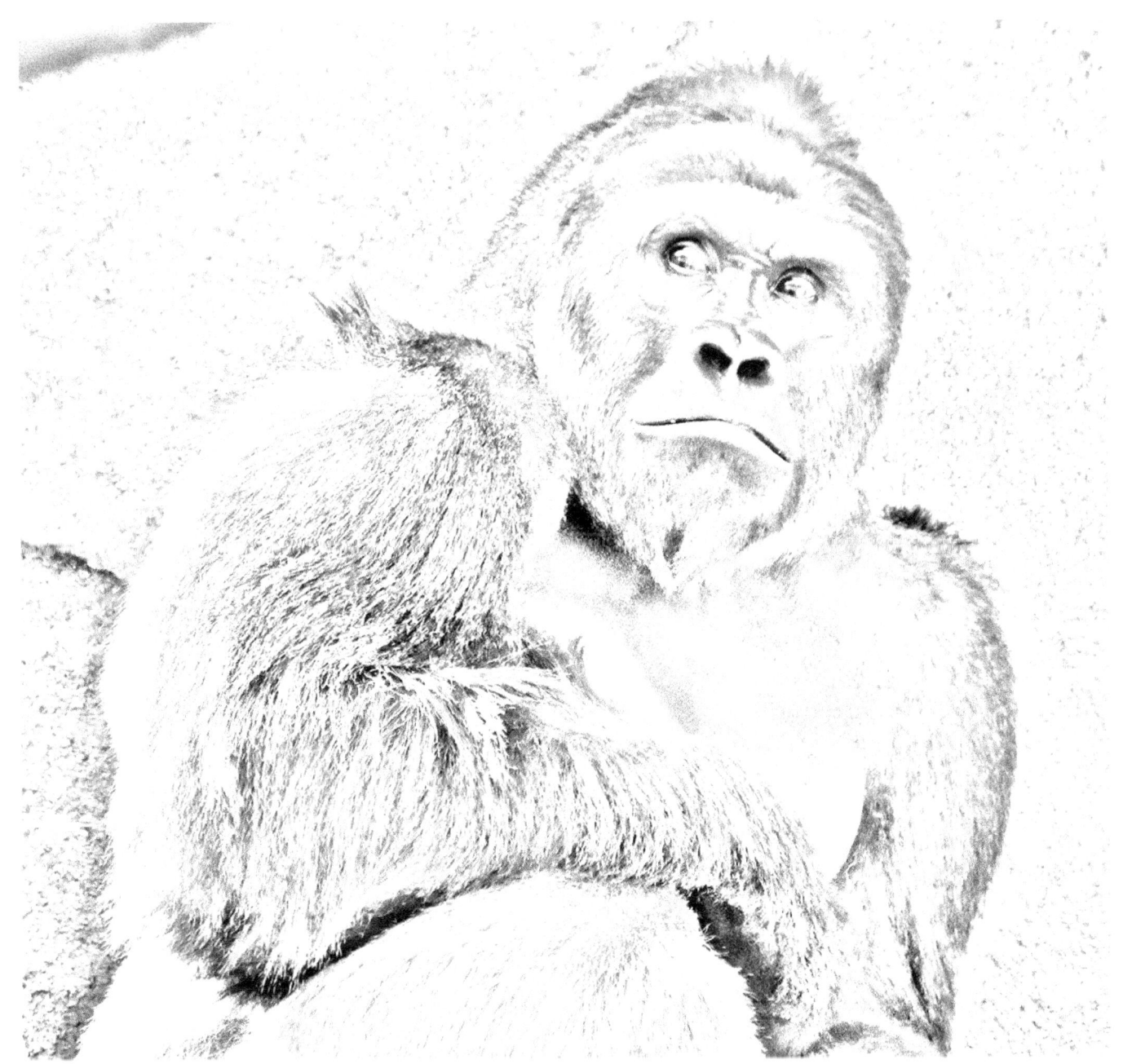

HARAMBE

VIEWED BY THOUSANDS OF VISITORS EACH YEAR

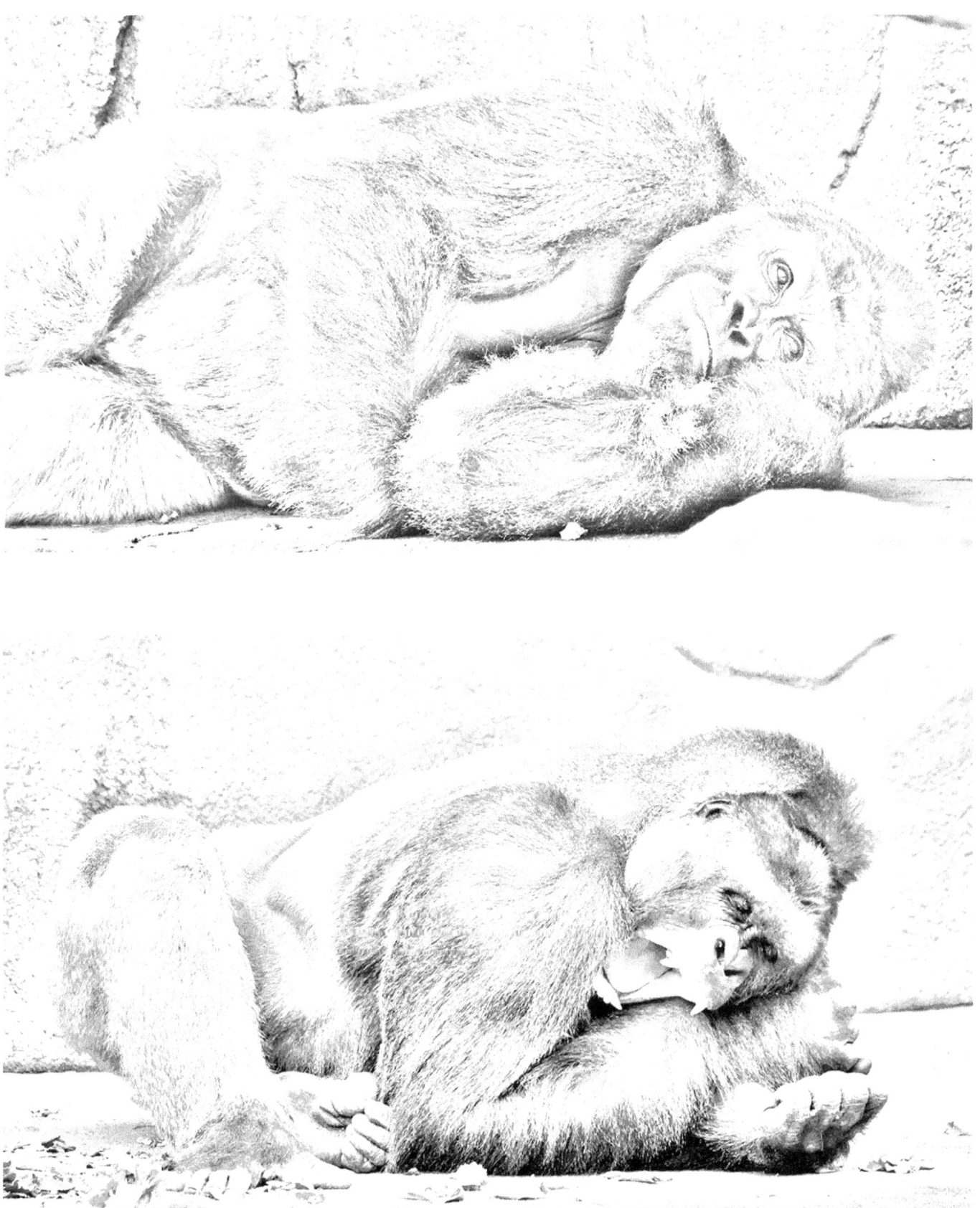

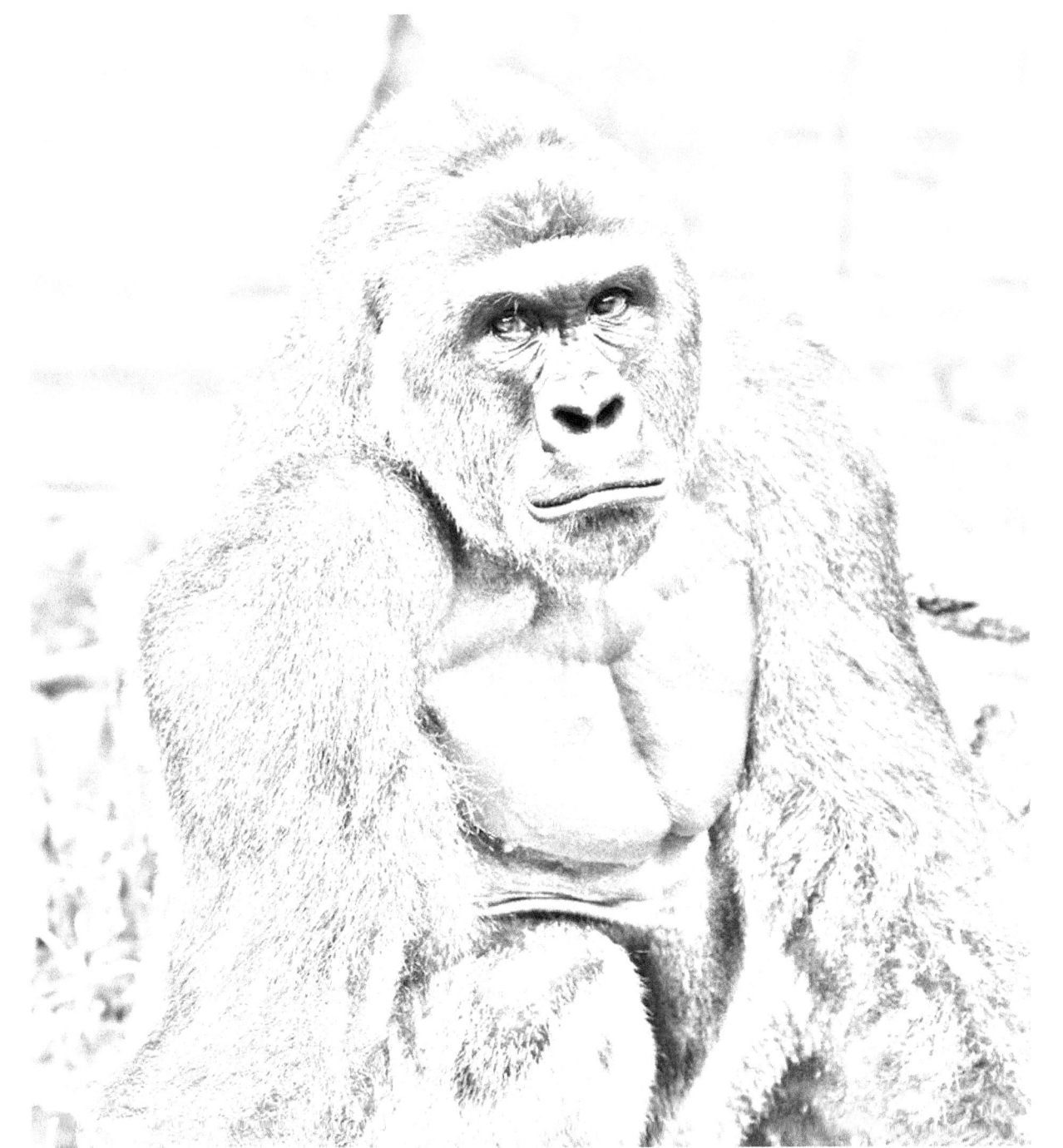

HARAMBE

Born at Gladys Porter Zoo in Brownsville, Texas

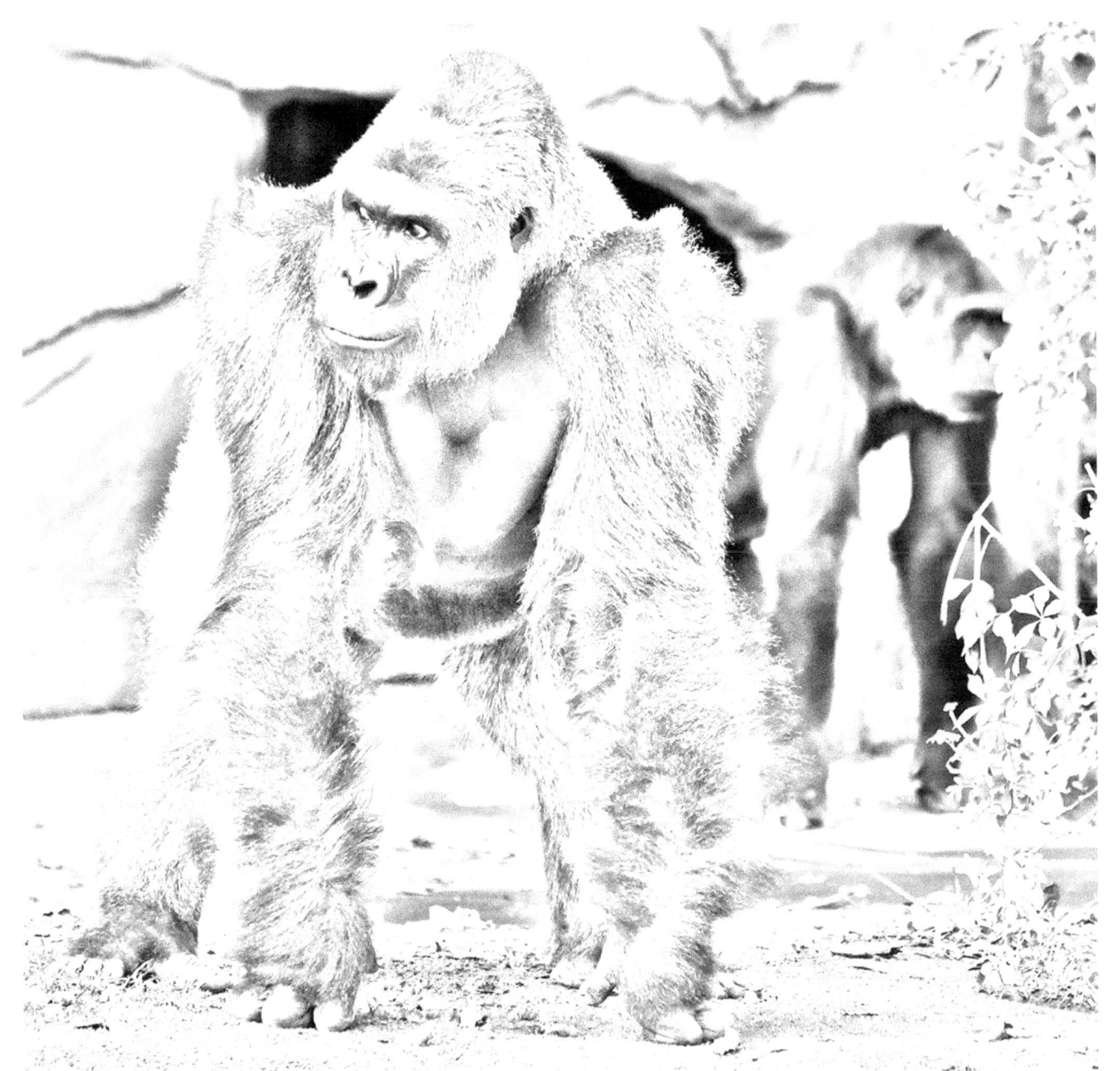

HARAMBE

BIRTHDAY IS MAY 27, 1999

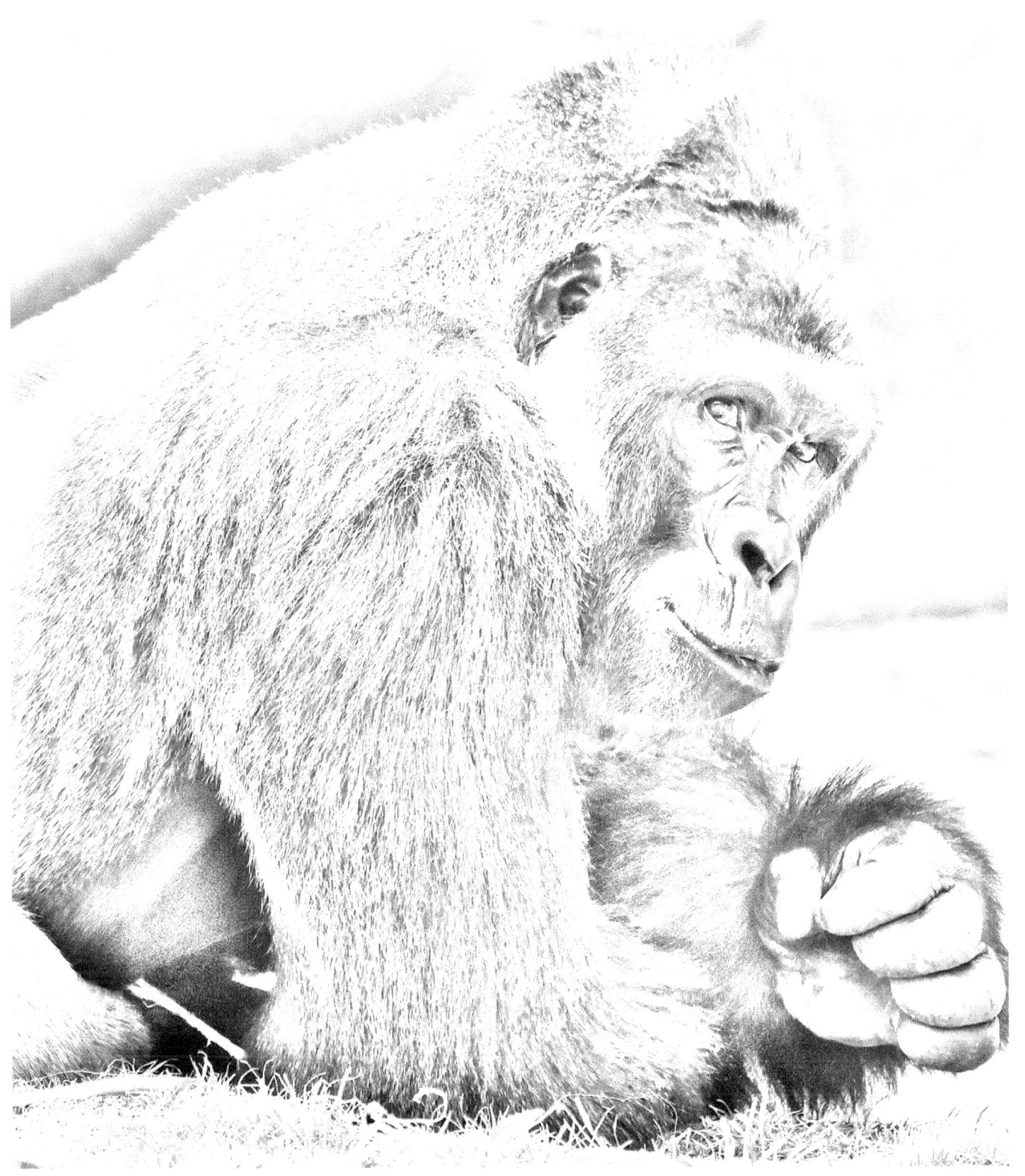

HARAMBE

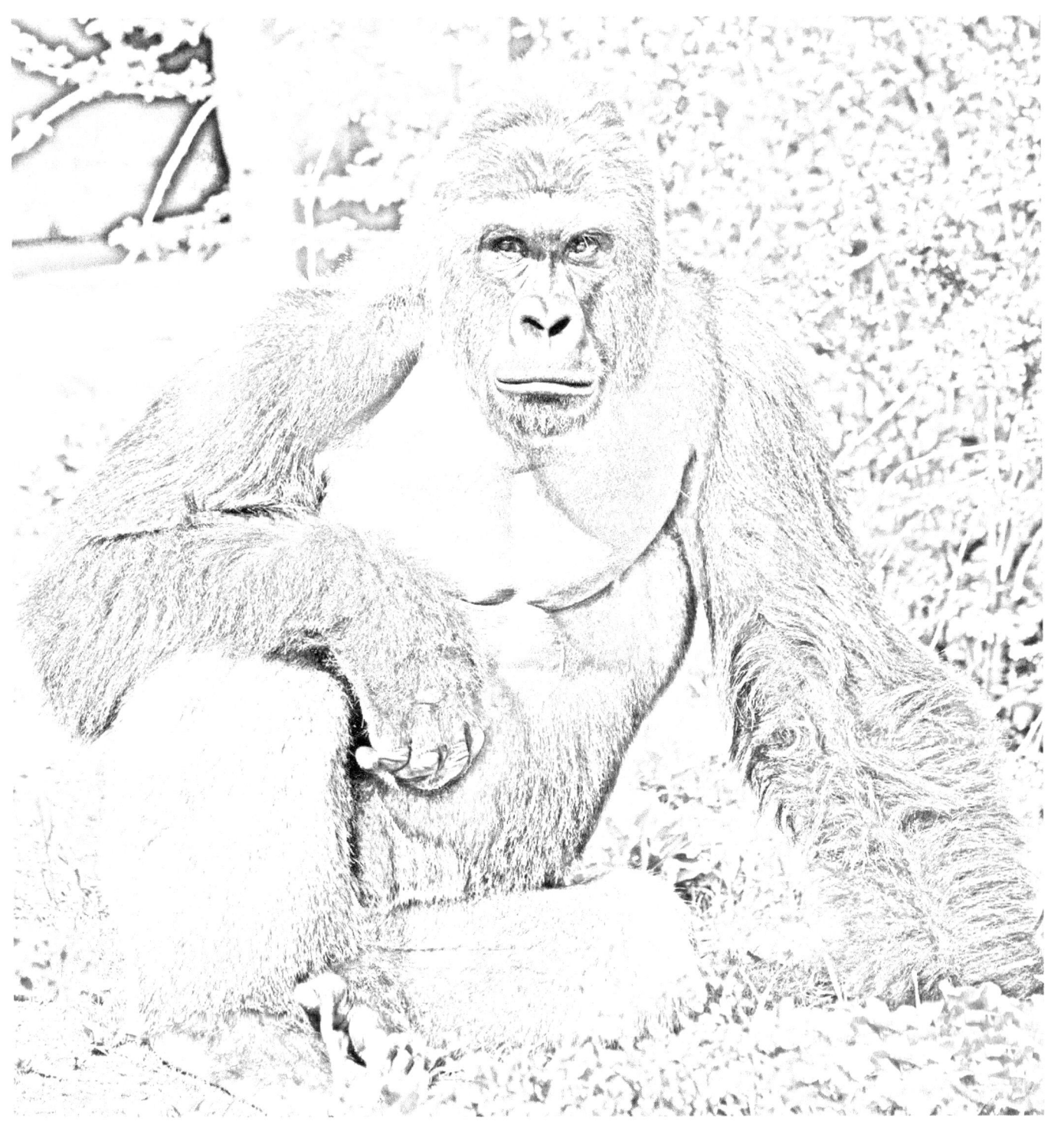

HARAMBE

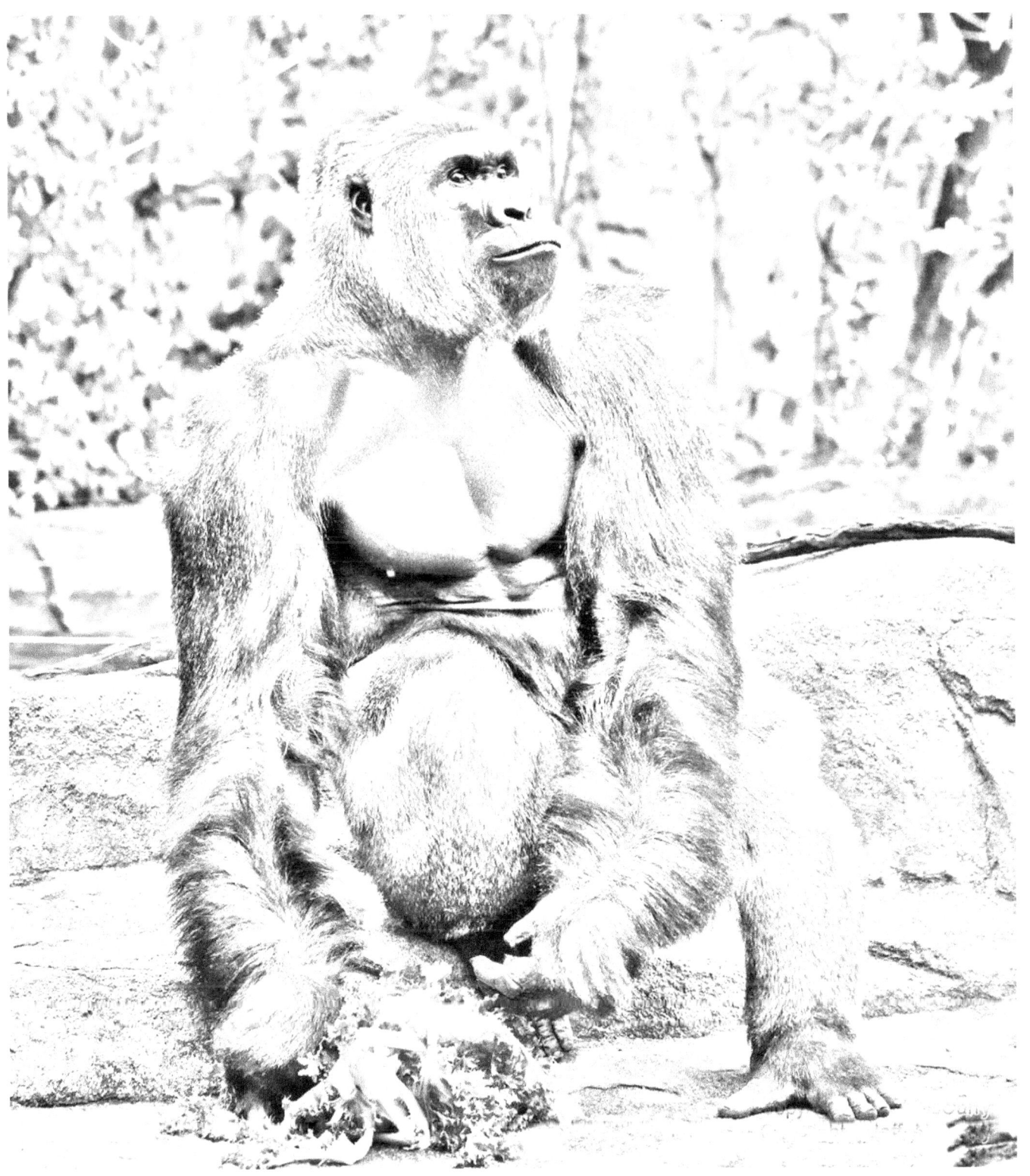

HARAMBE

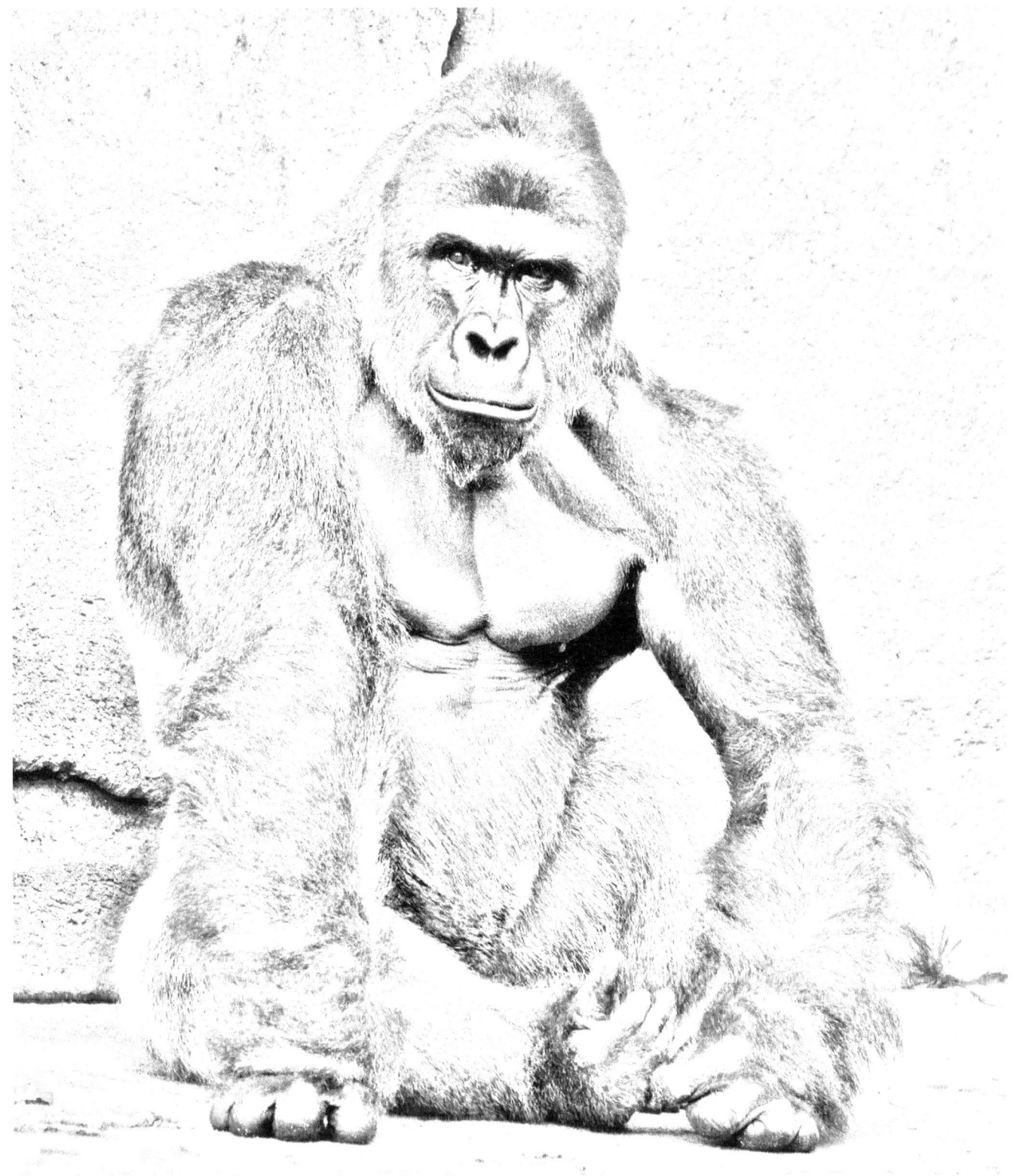

HARAMBE

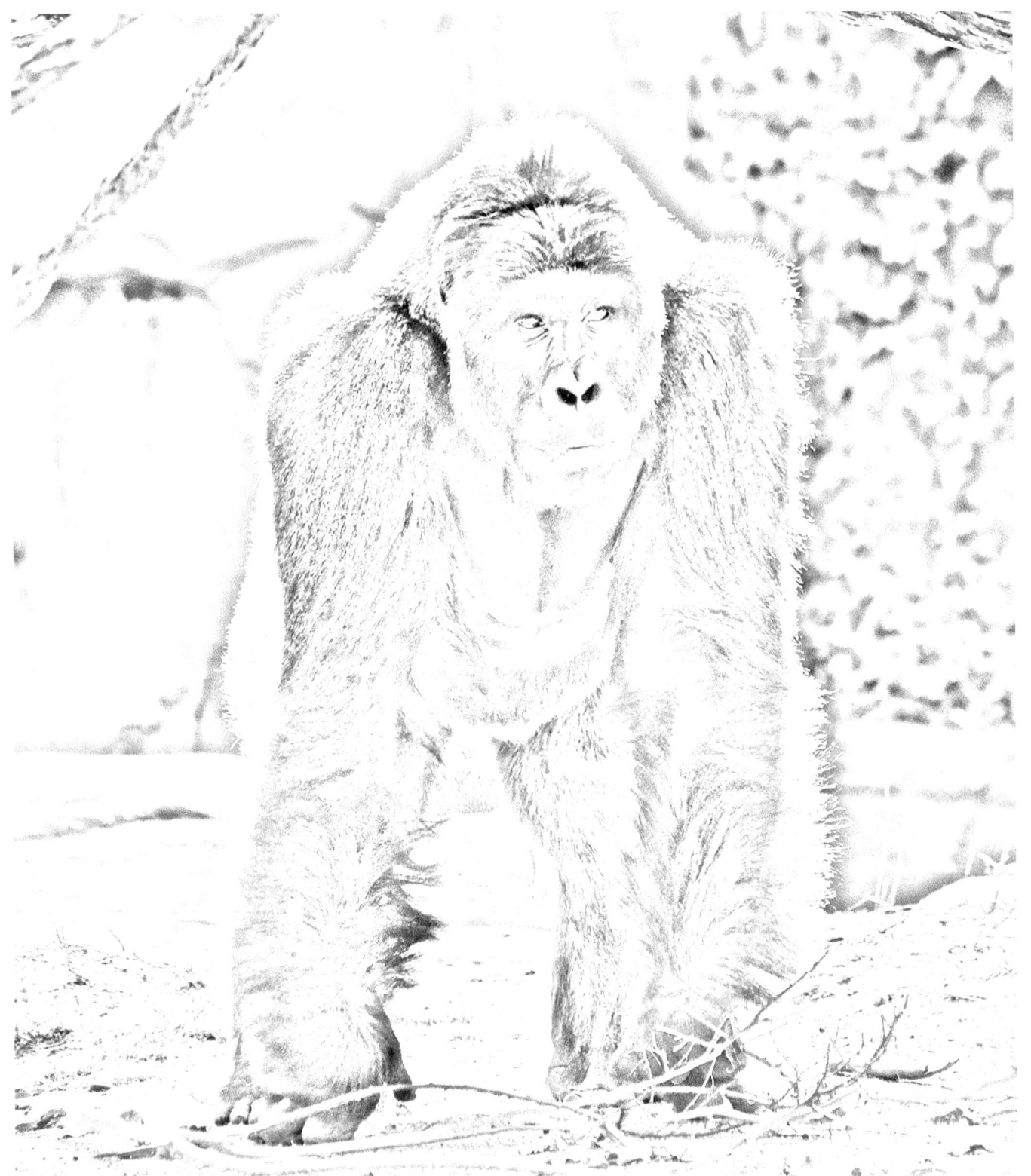

HARAMBE

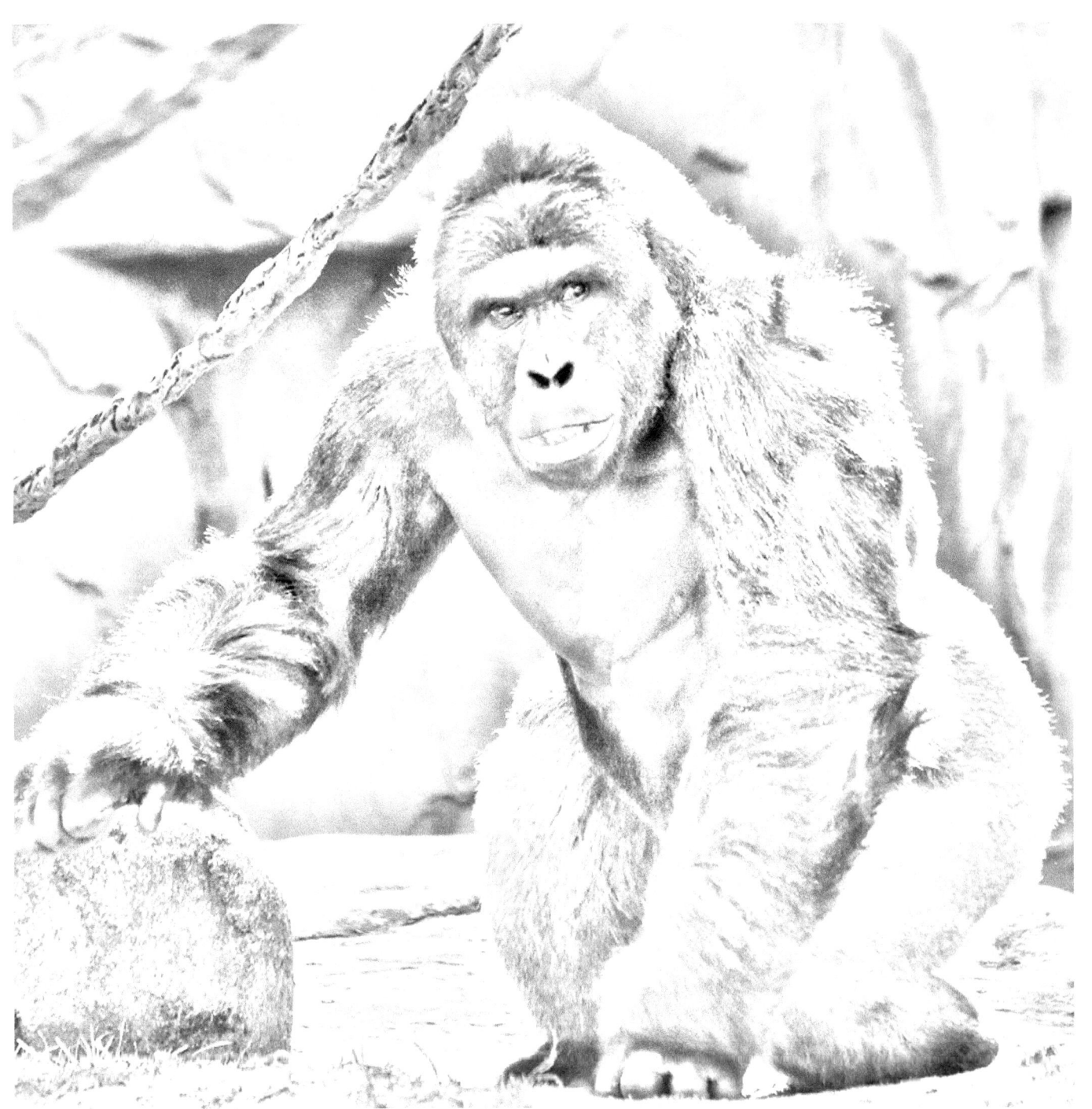

HARAMBE

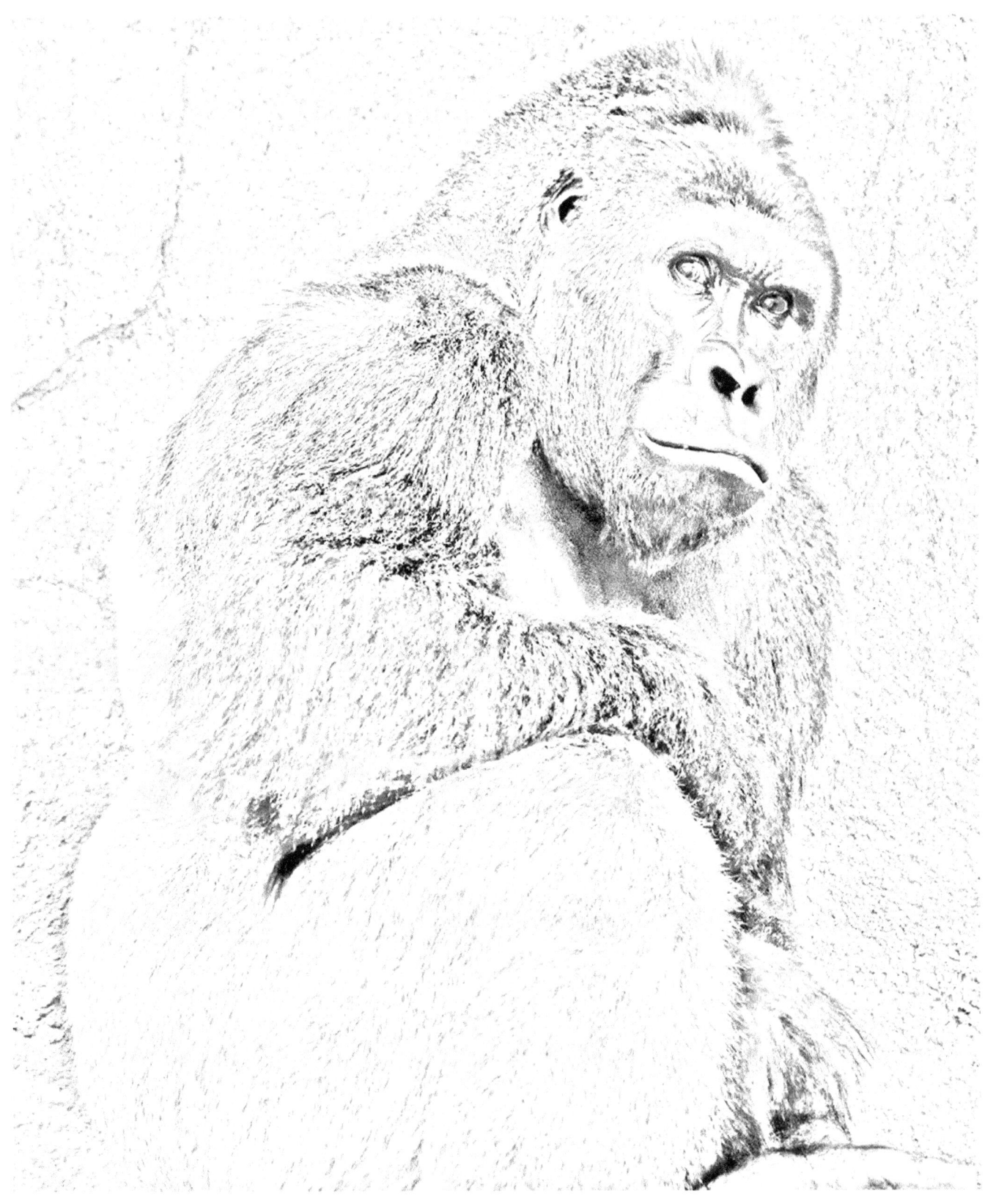

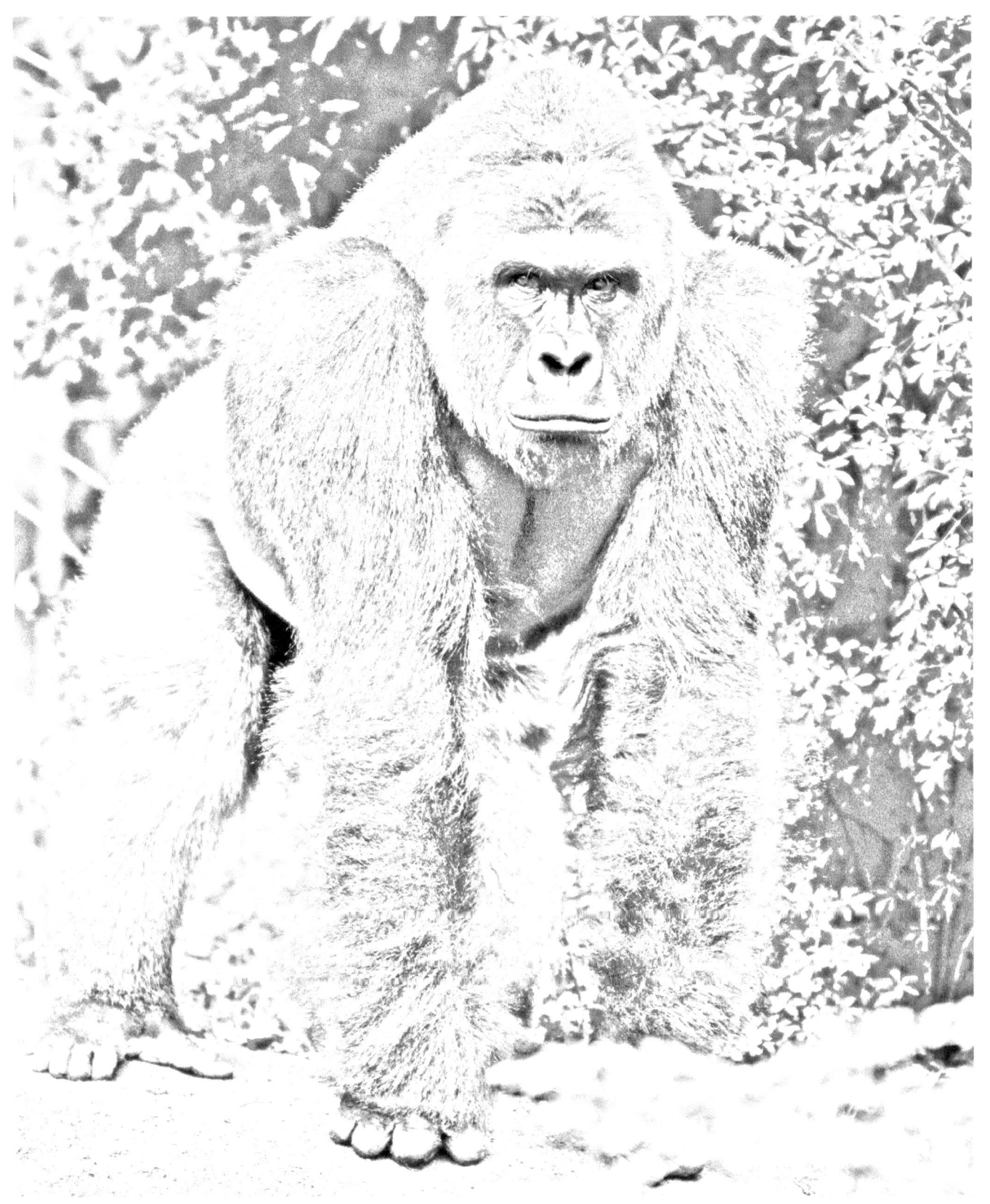

HARAMBE

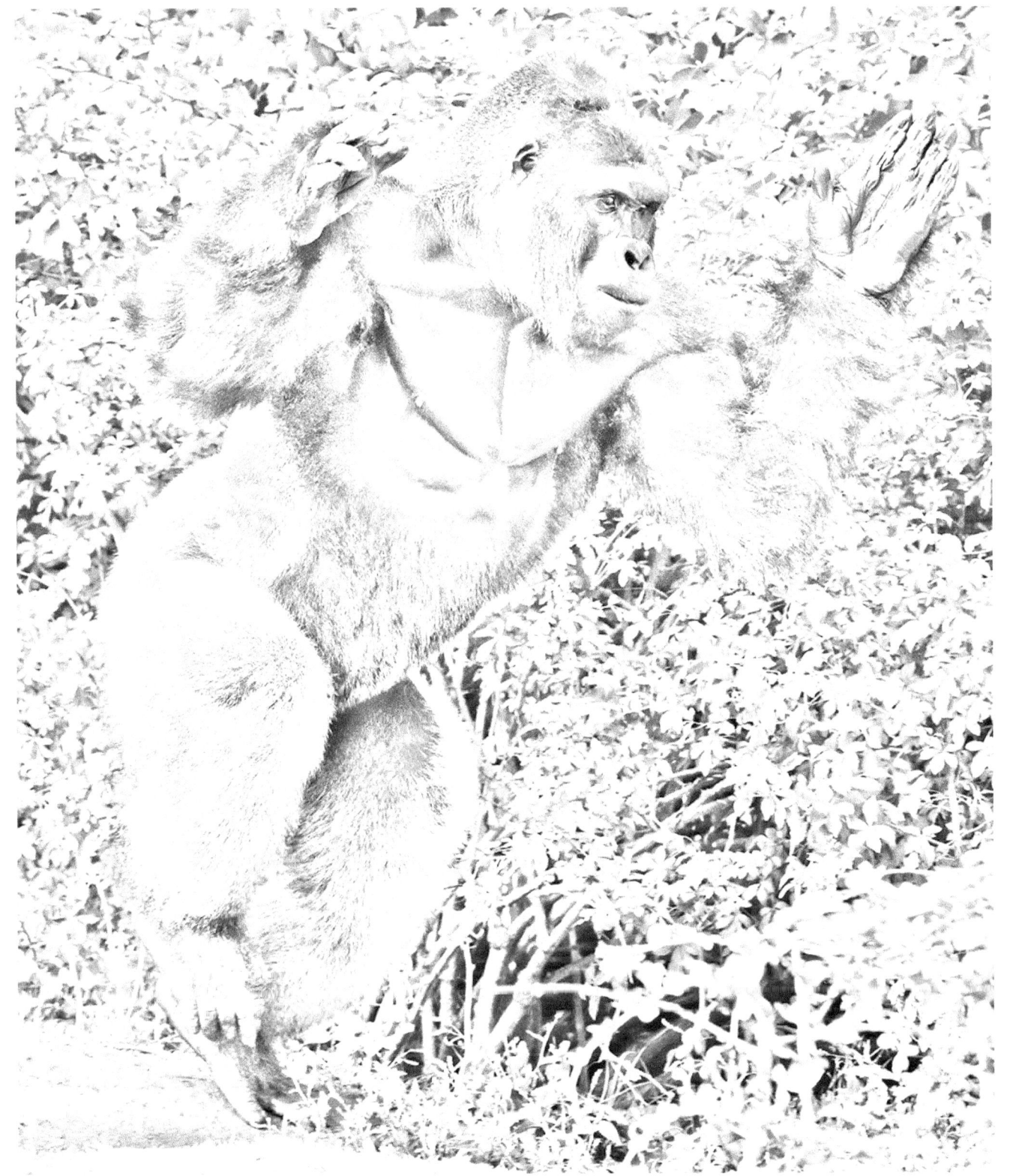

HARAMBE

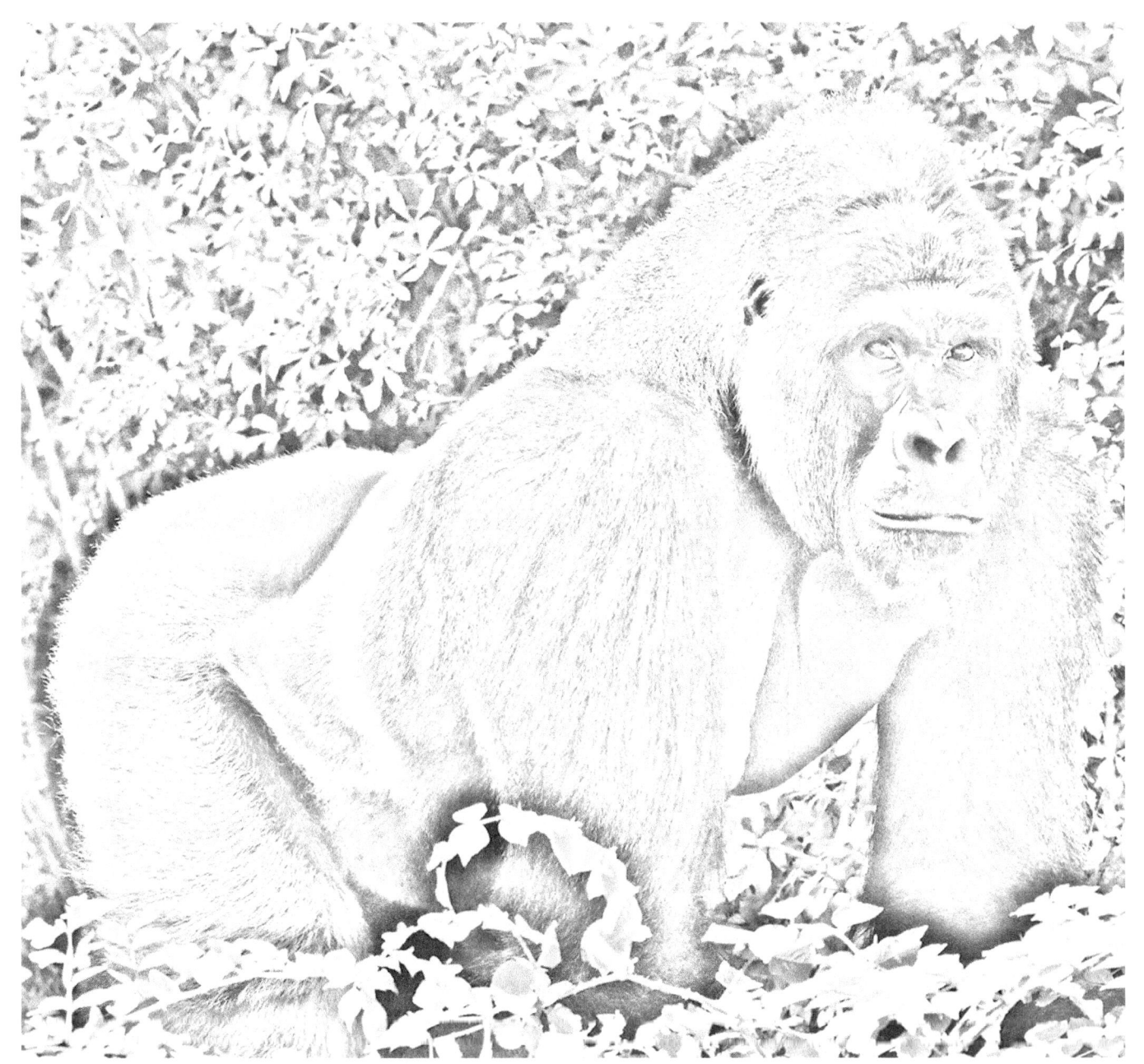

HARAMBE

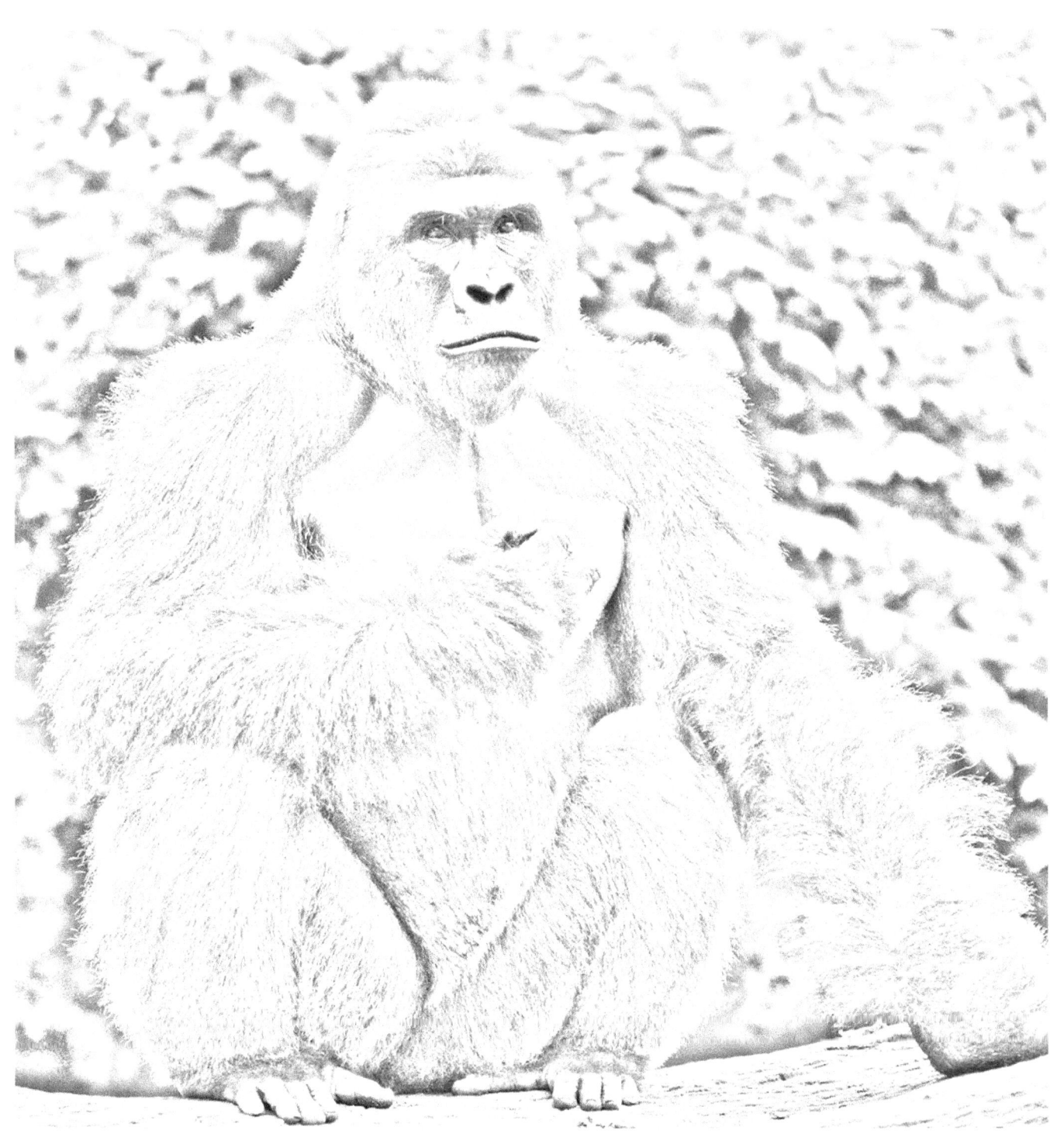

HARAMBE

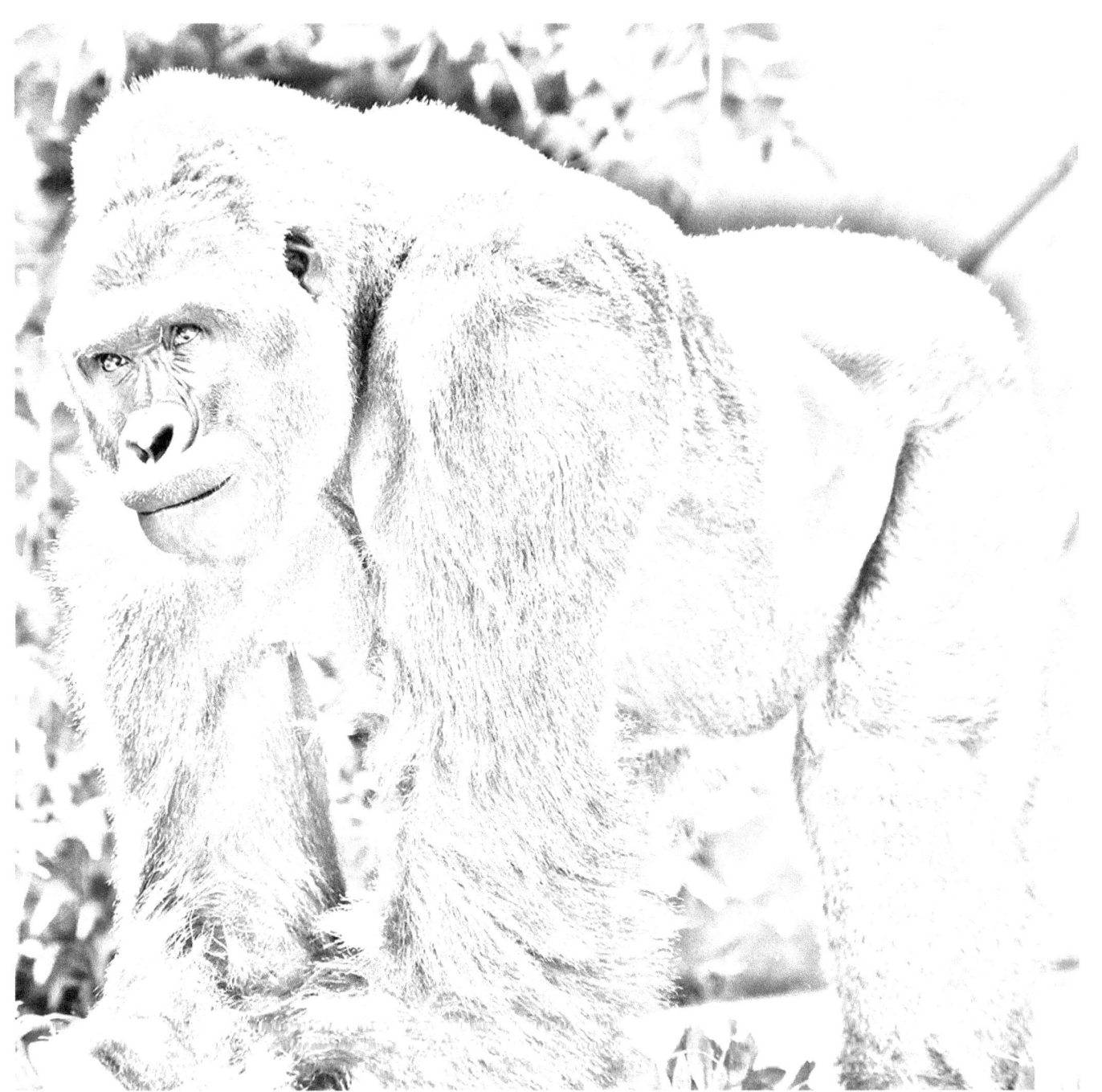

HARAMBE

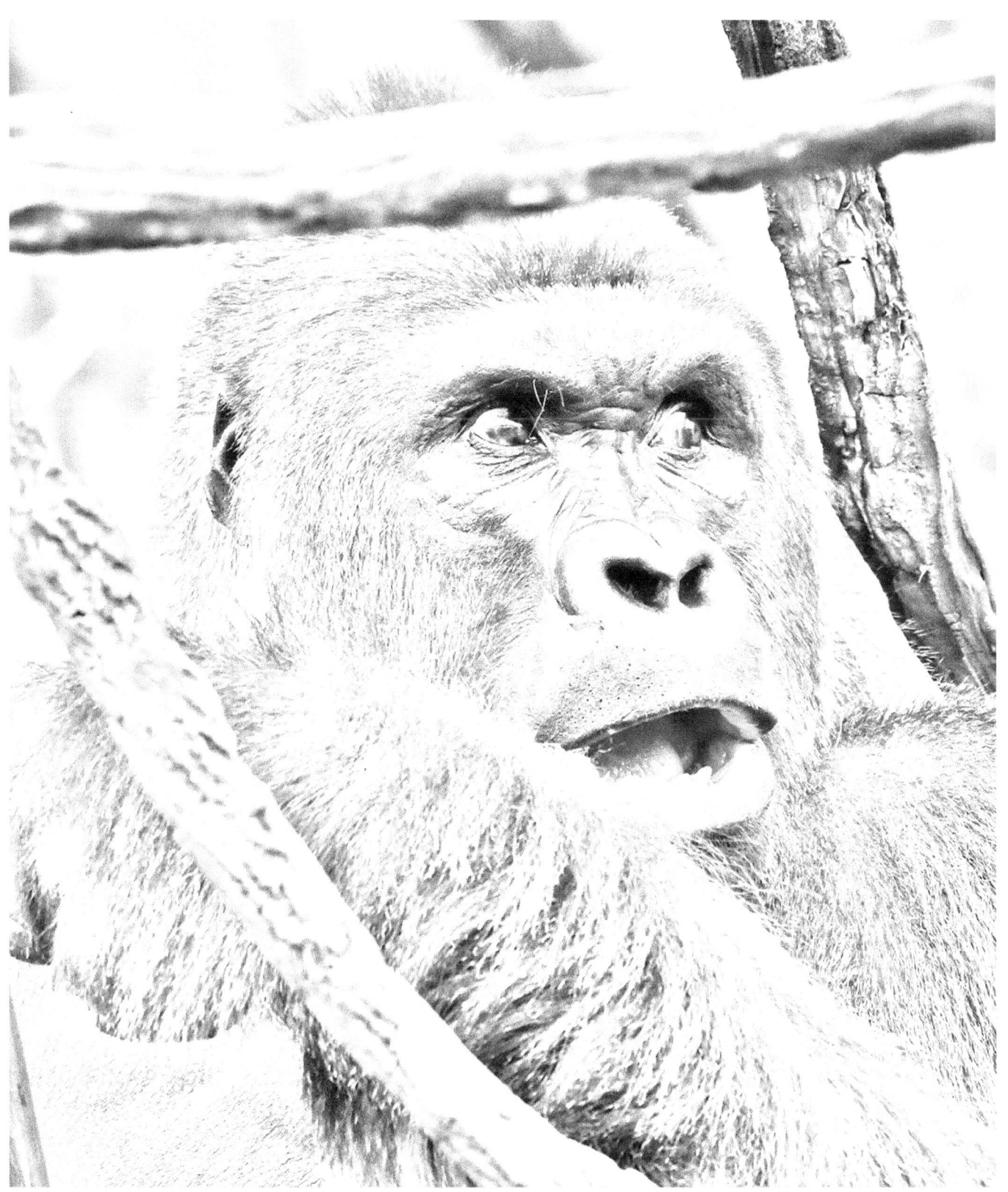

HARAMBE

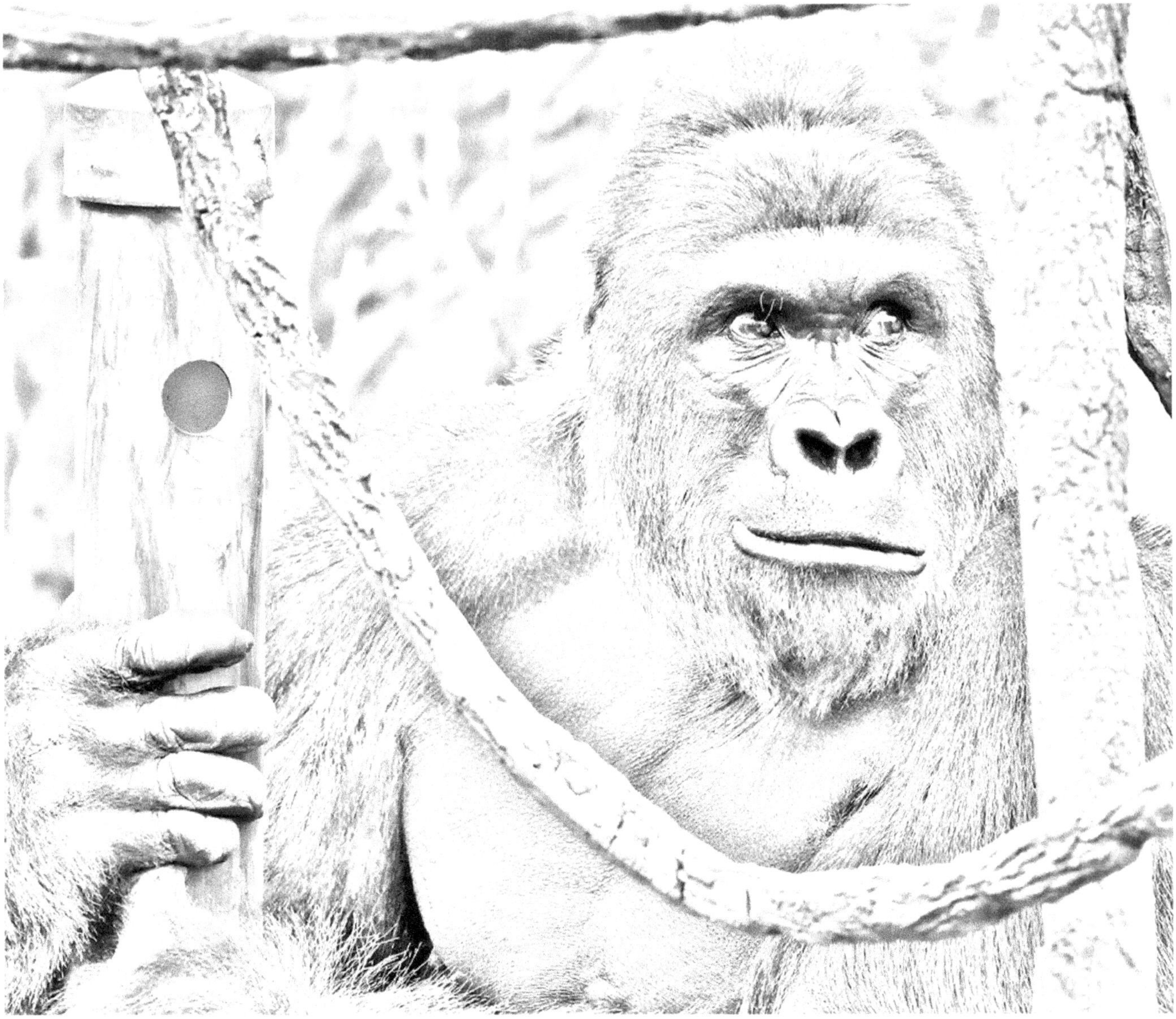

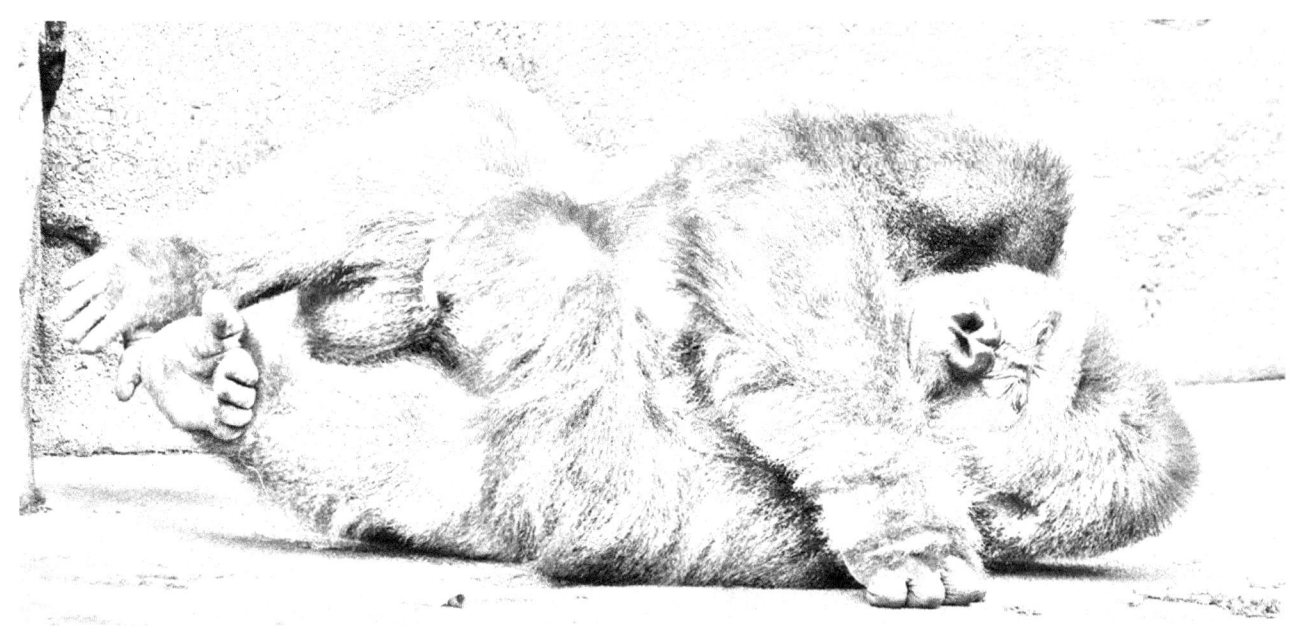

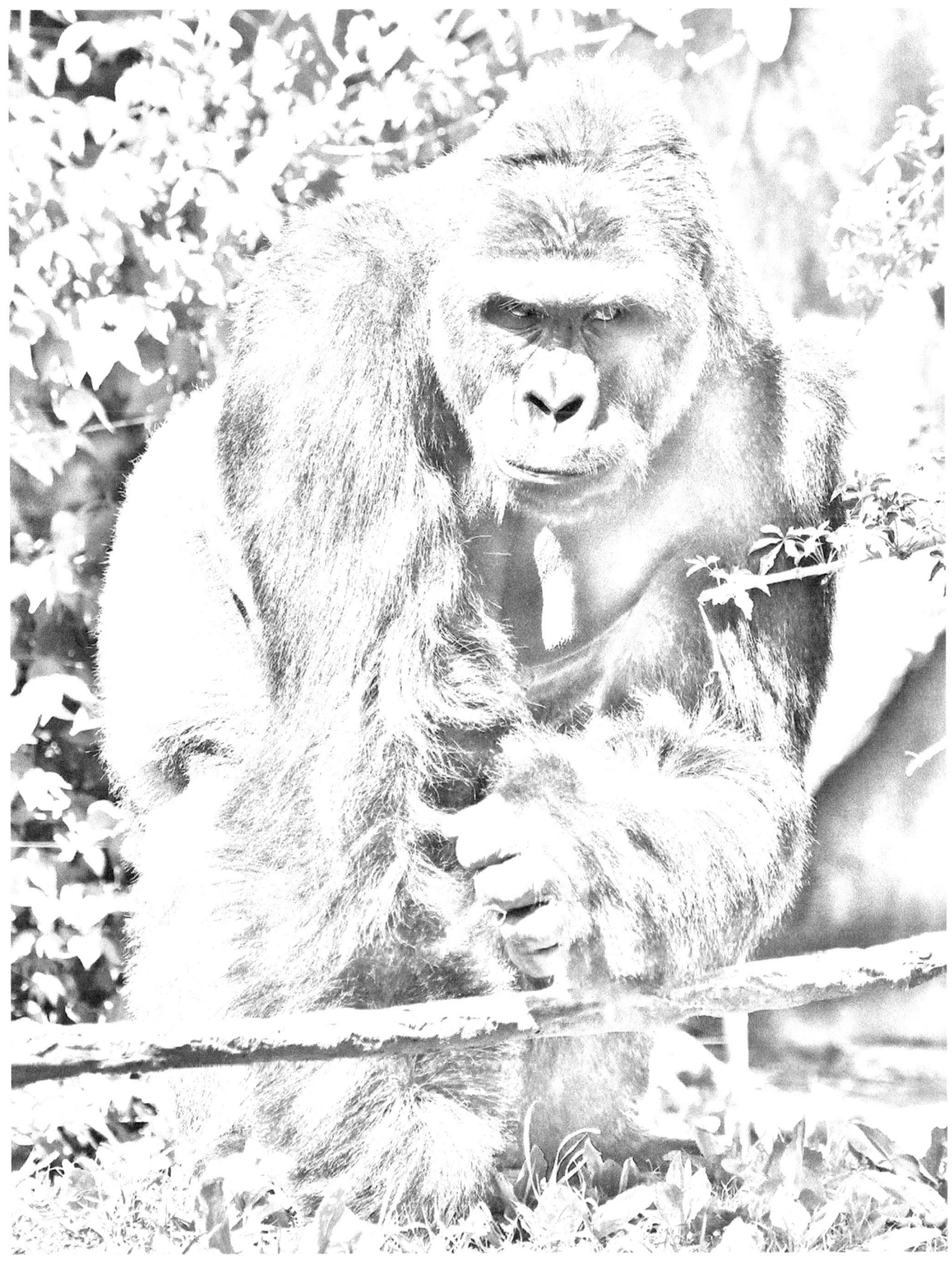

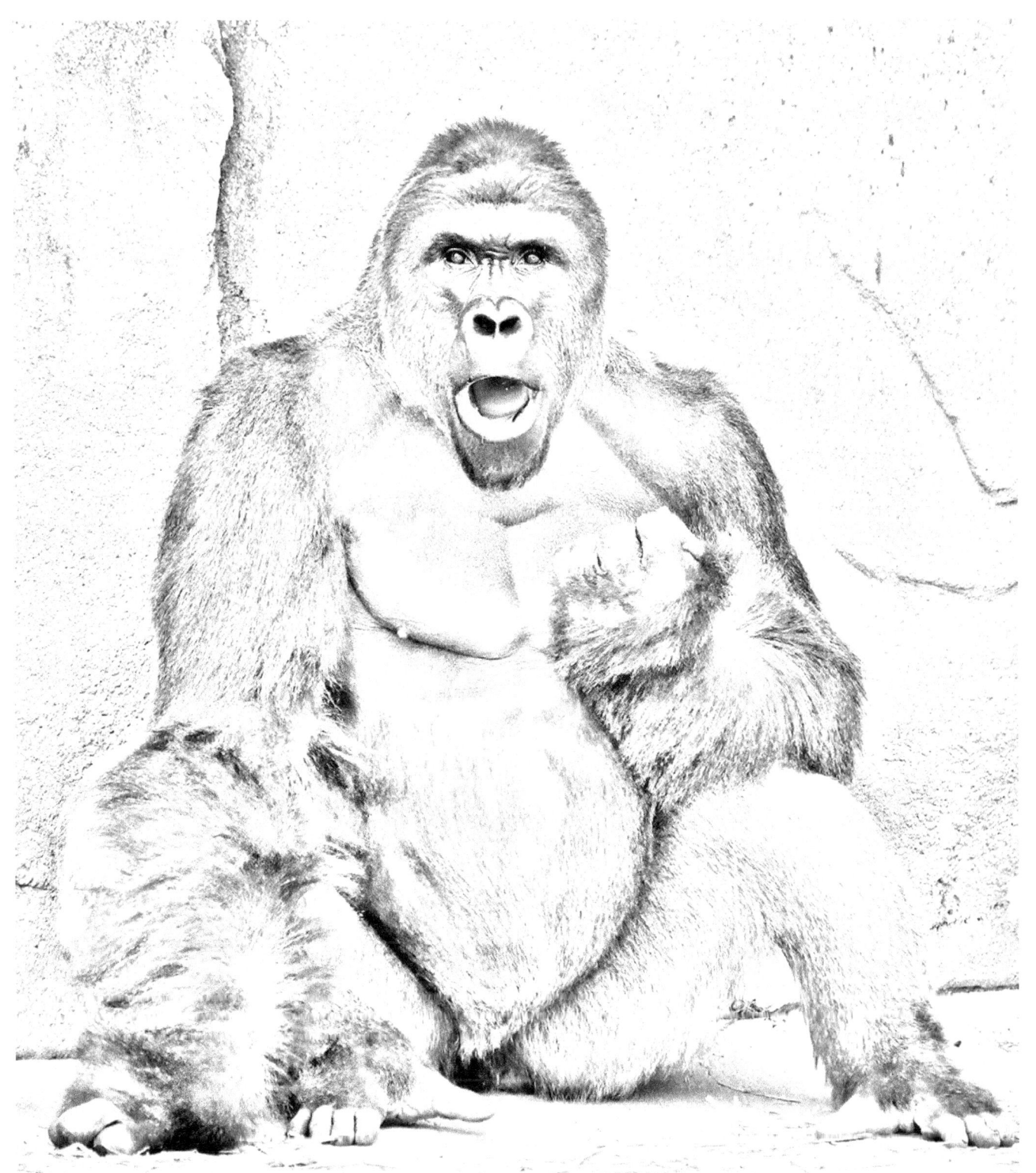

HARAMBE

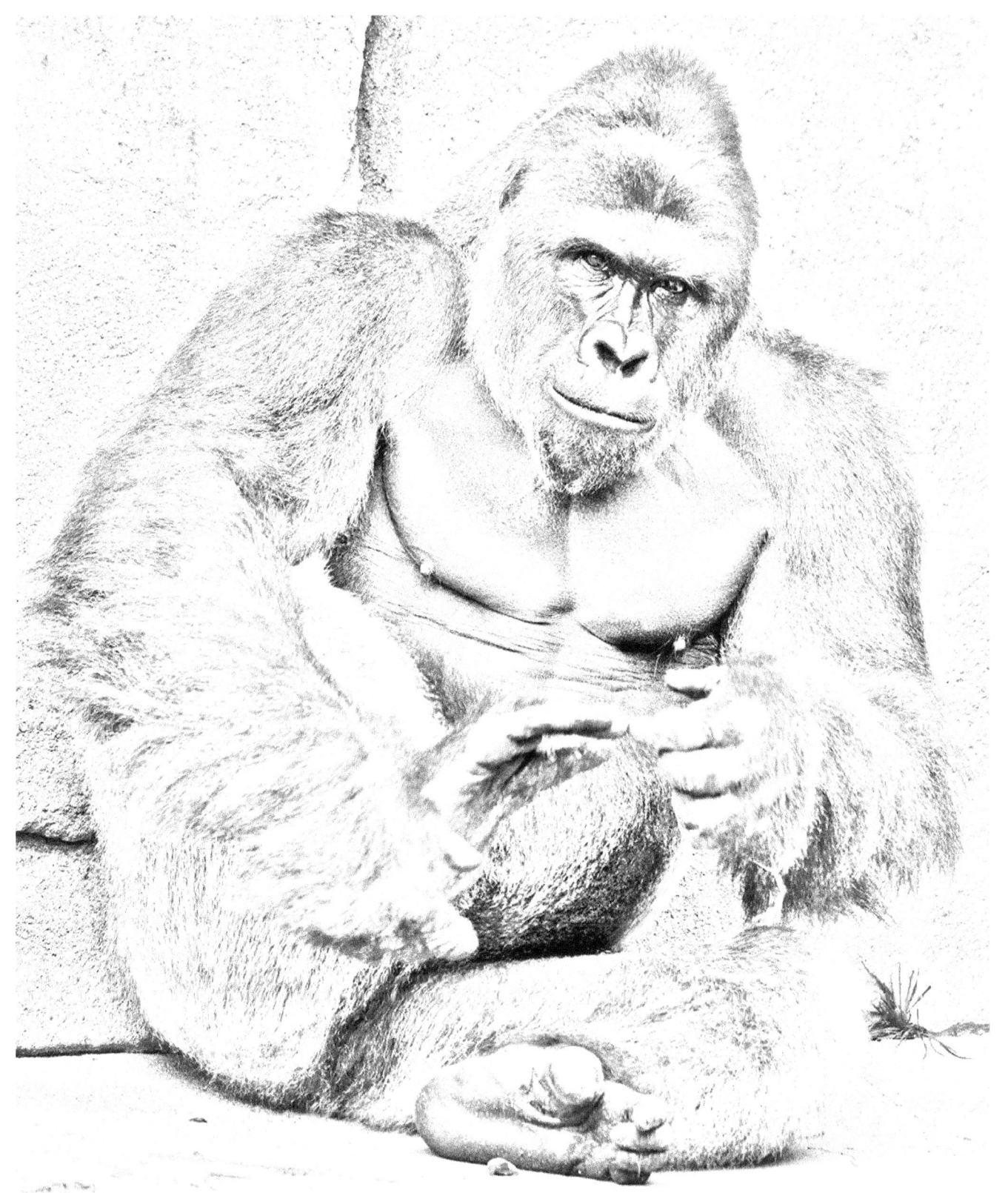

HARAMBE

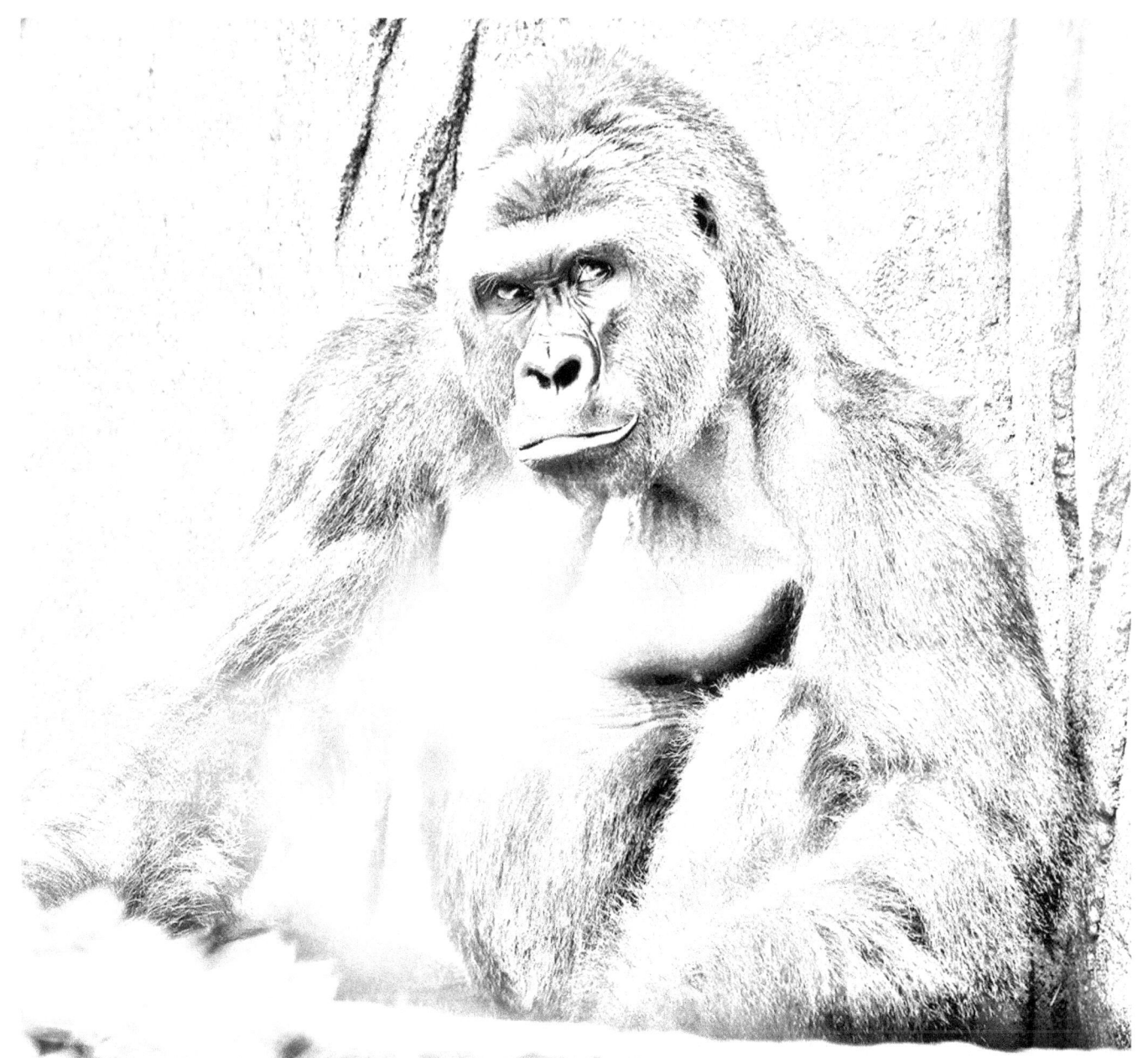

HARAMBE

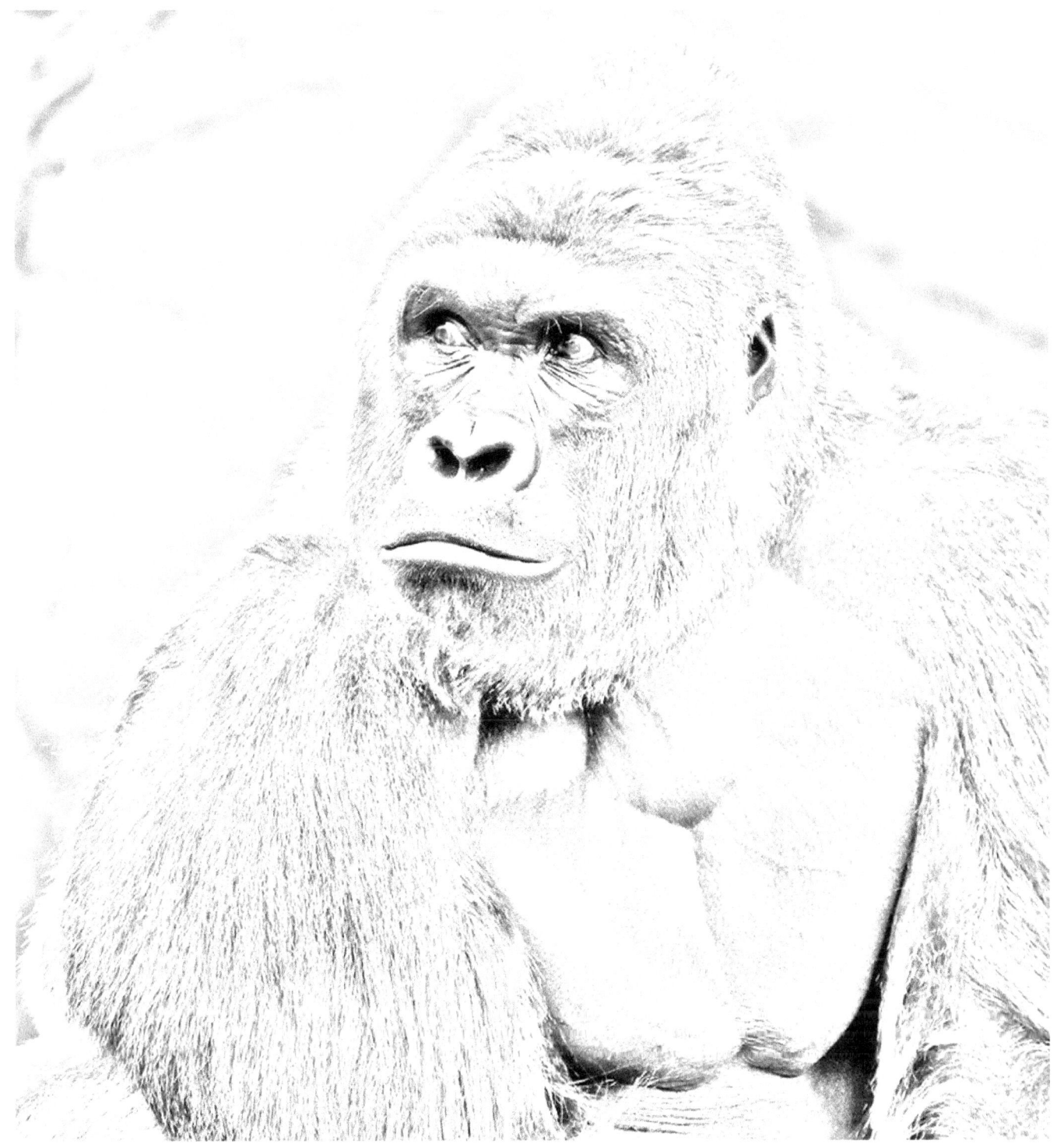

HARAMBE

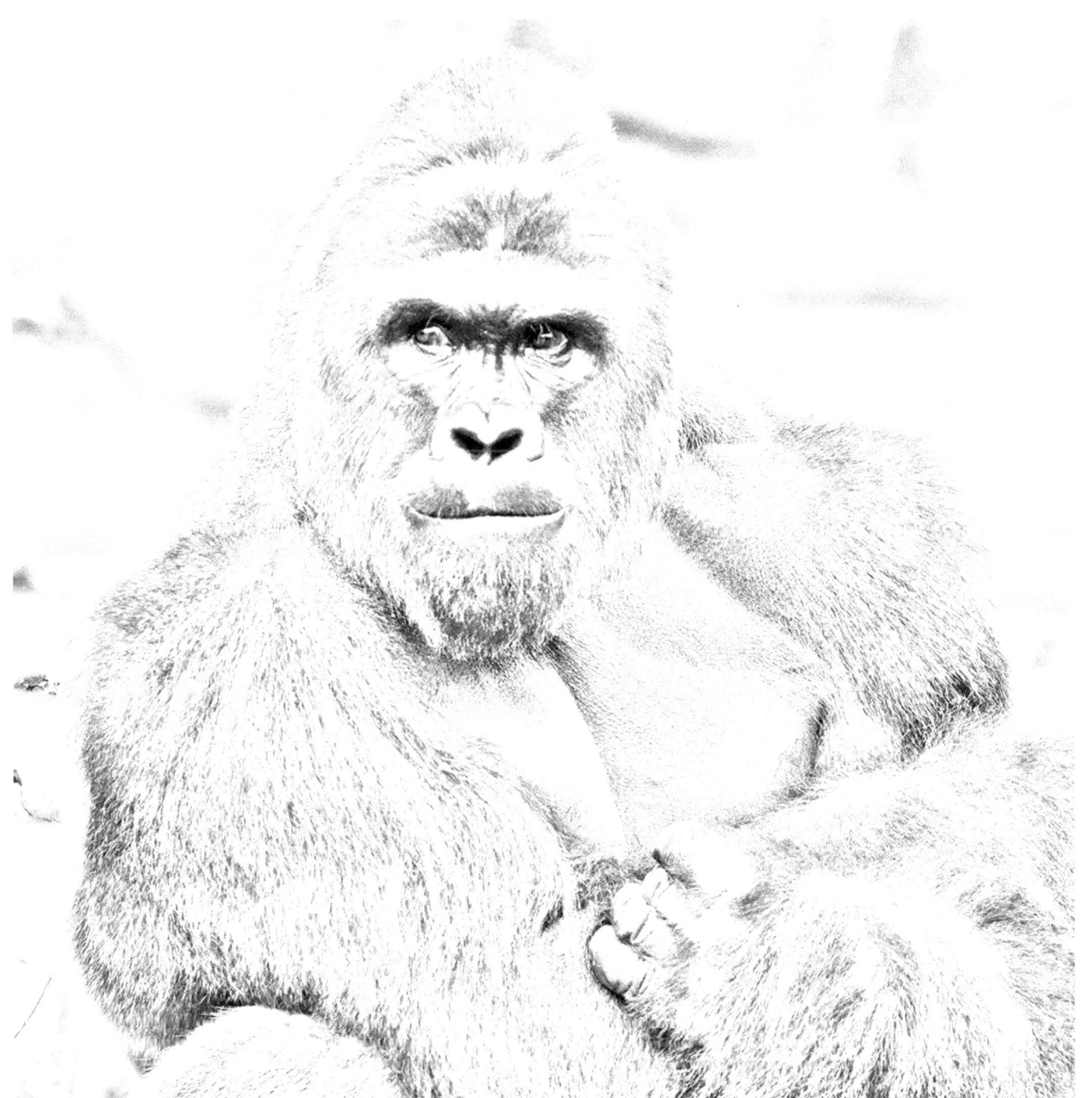

HARAMBE

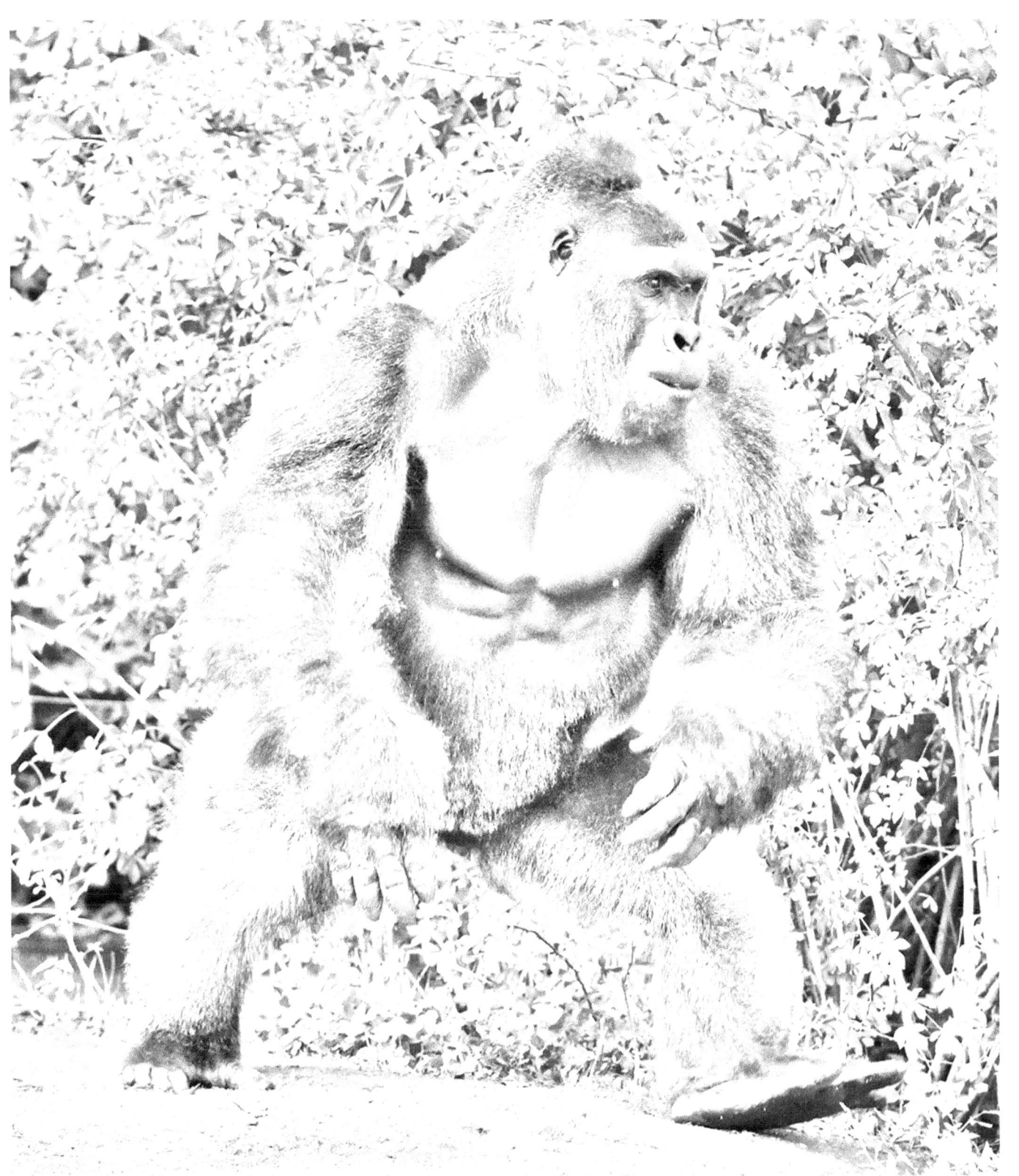

HARAMBE

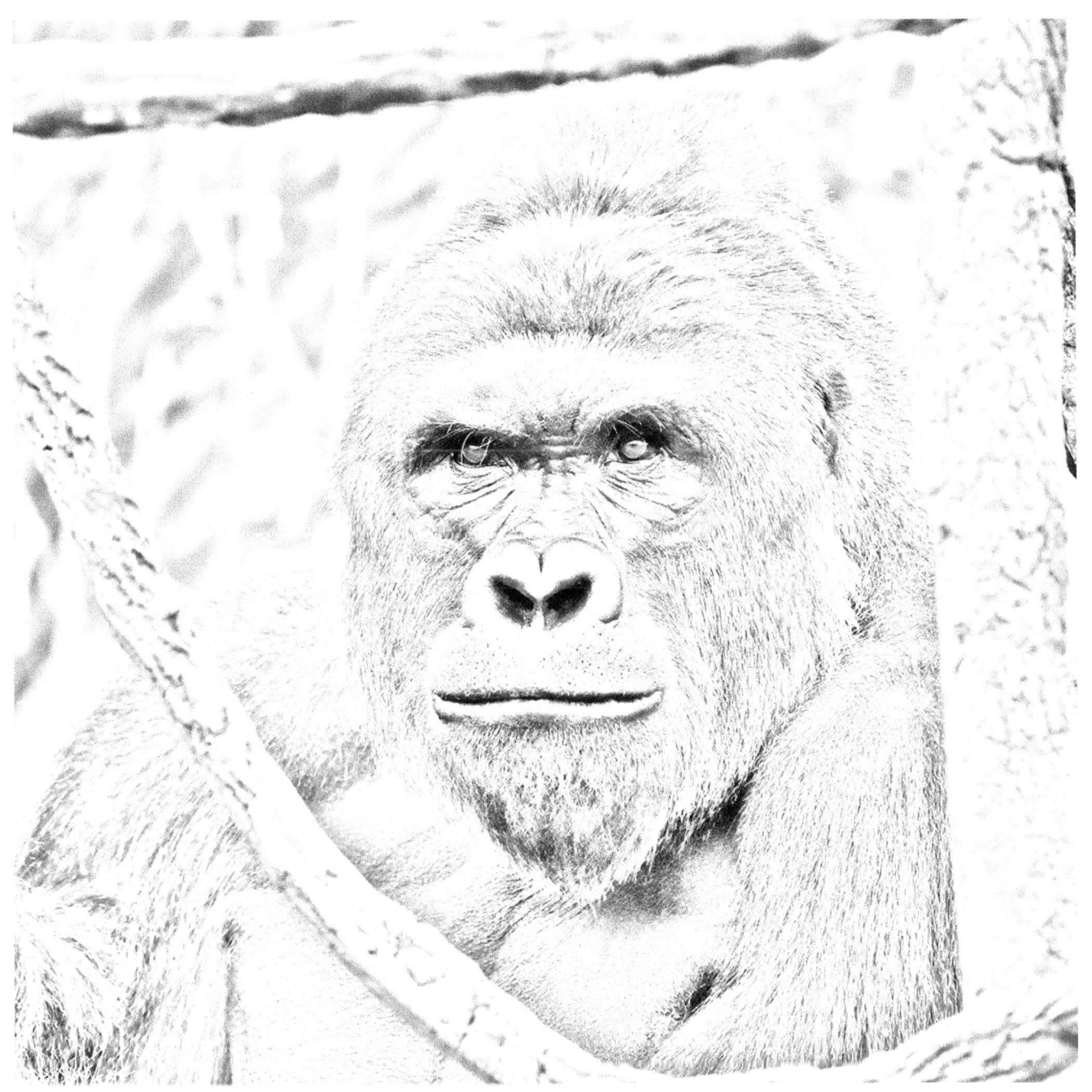

HARAMBE

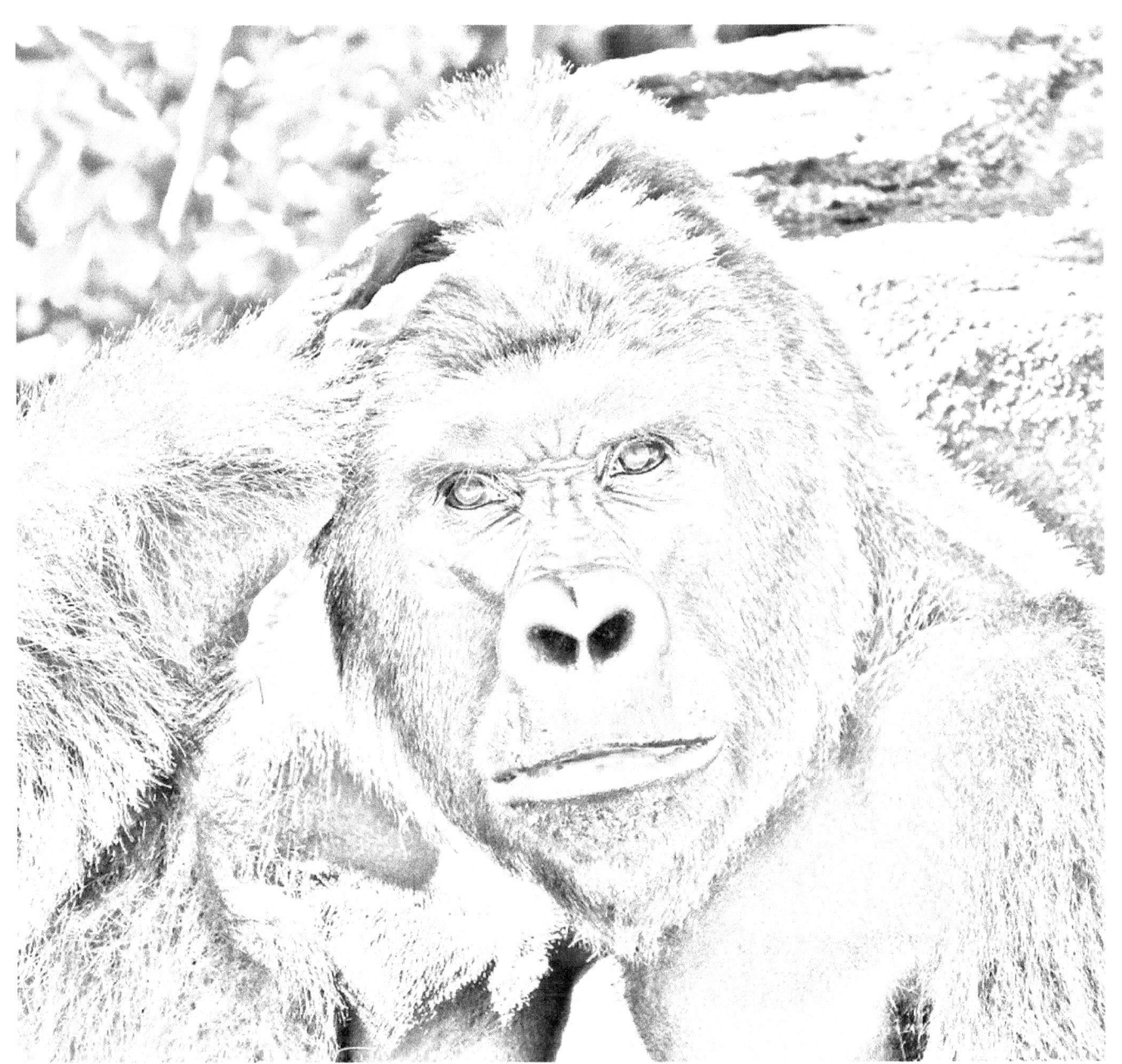

HARAMBE

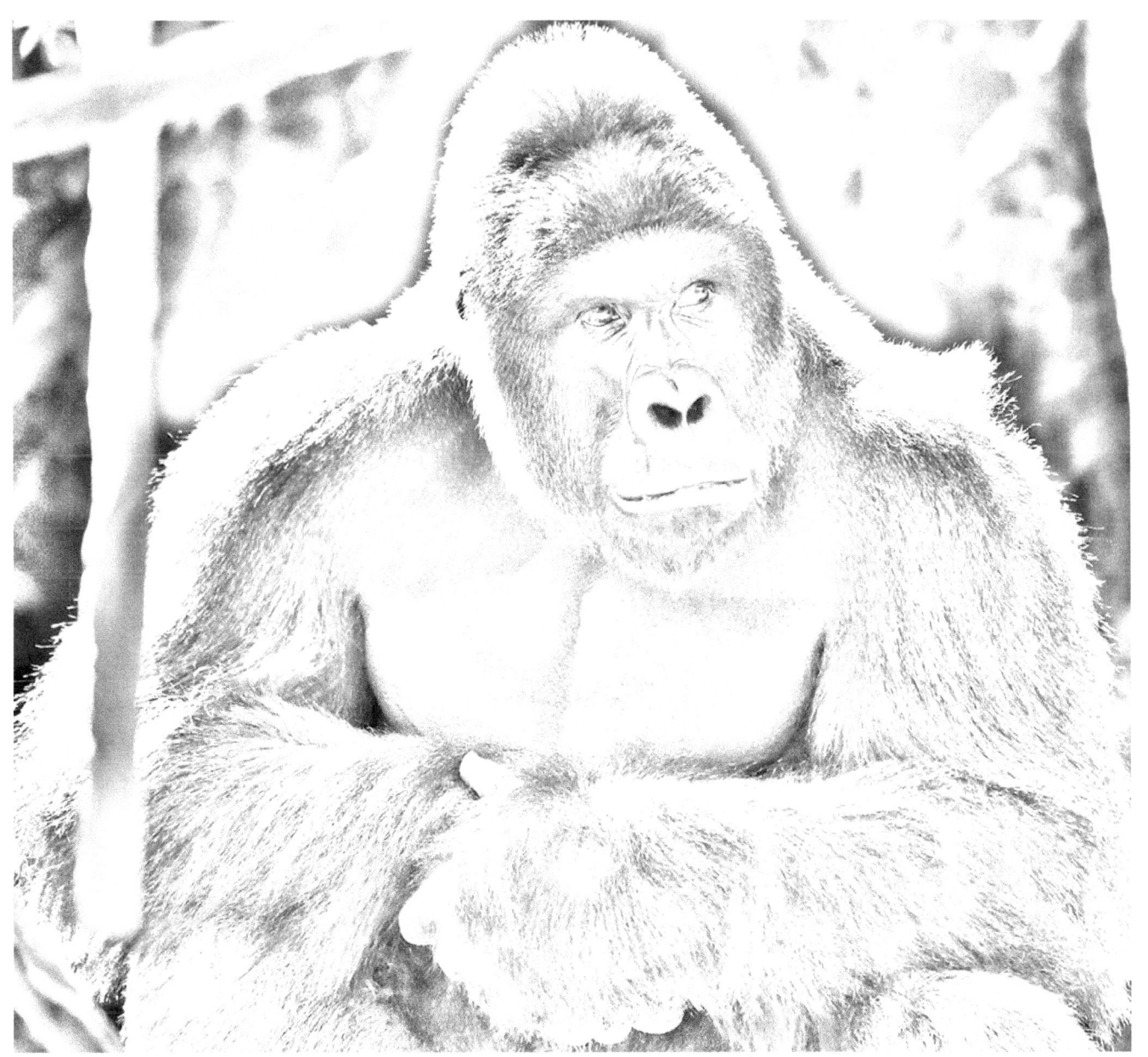

HARAMBE

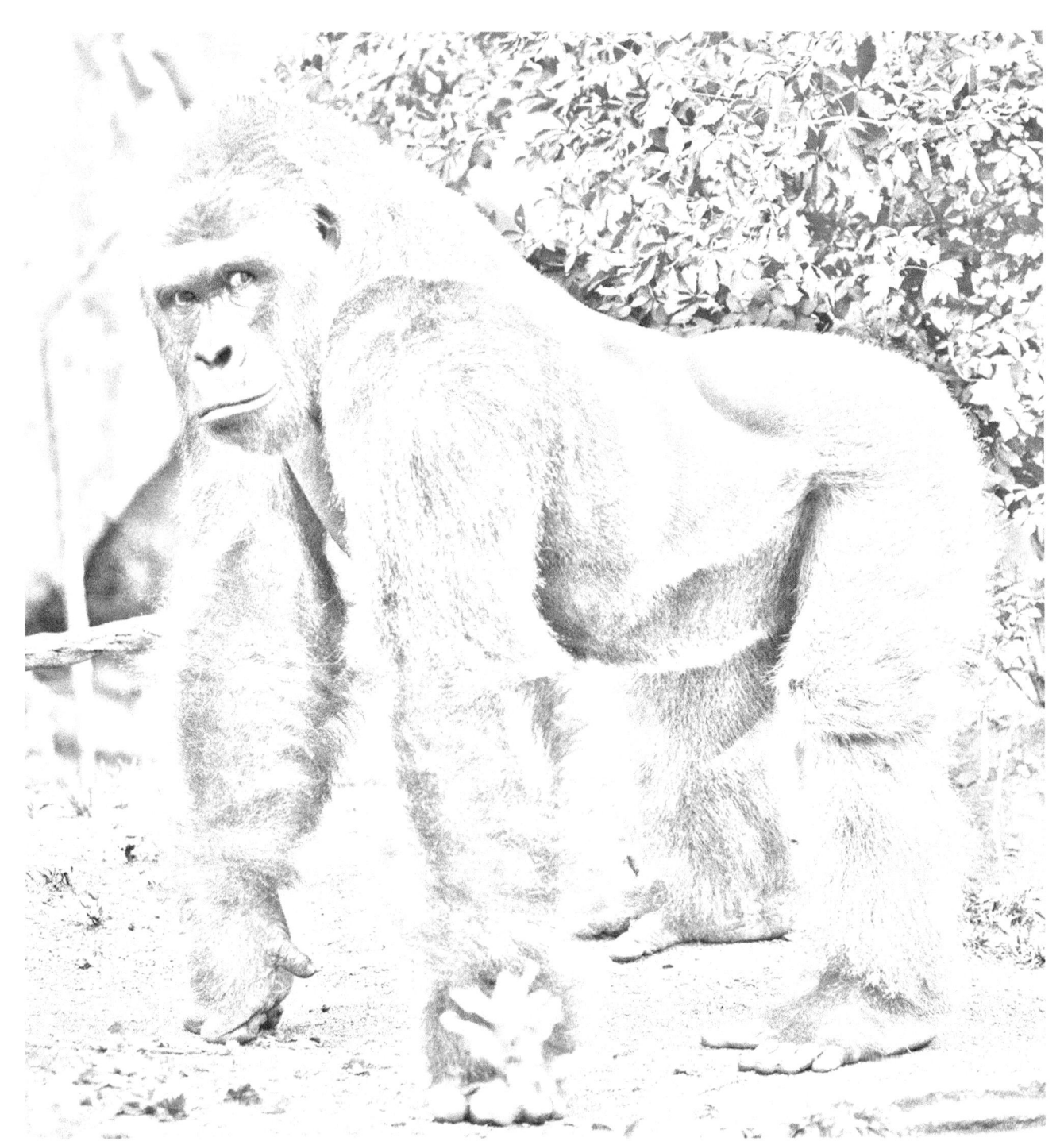

HARAMBE

IN MEMORIAM

MAY 28, 1999 - MAY 27, 2016

NOW ON SALE

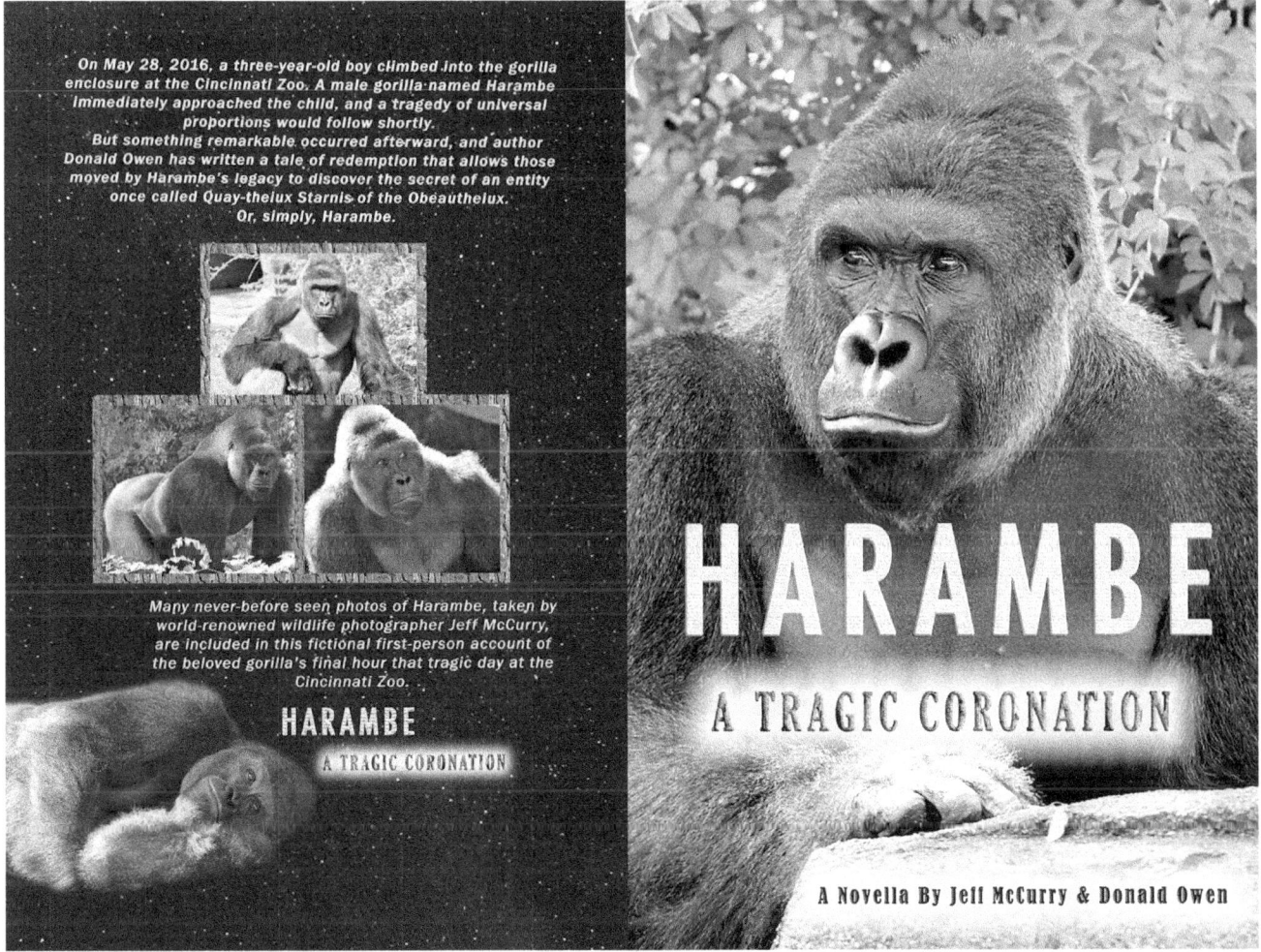

On May 28, 2016, a three-year-old boy climbed into the gorilla enclosure at the Cincinnati Zoo. A male gorilla named Harambe immediately approached the child, and a tragedy of universal proportions would follow shortly.

But something remarkable occurred afterward, and author Donald Owen has written a tale of redemption that allows those moved by Harambe's legacy to discover the secret of an entity once called Quay-theiux Starnis of the Obeautheiux.

Or, simply, Harambe.

Many never-before seen photos of Harambe, taken by world-renowned wildlife photographer Jeff McCurry, are included in this fictional first-person account of the beloved gorilla's final hour that tragic day at the Cincinnati Zoo.

HARAMBE
A TRAGIC CORONATION

HARAMBE
A TRAGIC CORONATION

A Novella By Jeff McCurry & Donald Owen

Dr. Jenny Blundell is a Texas-based ophthalmologist with degrees from Harvard and Johns Hopkins. She has traveled the world and helped countless numbers of patients with their sight.

But Jenny saw something as a 12-year-old in 1983 that has produced an extraordinary spiritual convergence in the present between herself, a photographer named Jeff, and a silverback gorilla called Harambe. The visions from 1983 are found in a series of sketches Jenny drew as a seventh-grader, when she became withdrawn from her family and classmates because of a horrific situation involving a well-respected teacher.

Now the flashbacks from that episode have led Jenny to an animal she sketched thirty-three years earlier—even though the gorilla had not even been born. And the present-day realities have convinced Jenny that she is connected to Harambe in an eternal metempsychosis.

Her suspicions are confirmed following the tragic killing of Harambe, when she meets the photographer and learns of his near-death experience in 1985—something she foreshadowed in her sketches in 1983—and his unique bond with Harambe.

HARAMBE: A TRAGIC CORONATION is an 18,000-word novella that combines the first-person account of Harambe with the background story of Dr. Jenny Blundell, whose tale is shared through third-person vignettes. The novella also features the work and redemptive story of renowned wildlife photographer Jeff McCurry, who took thousands of pictures of Harambe while working at the Cincinnati Zoo. Many of McCurry's never-before seen photographs are included in the novella.

The novella is co-authored by McCurry and Donald Owen, and it is on sale at Amazon.com.

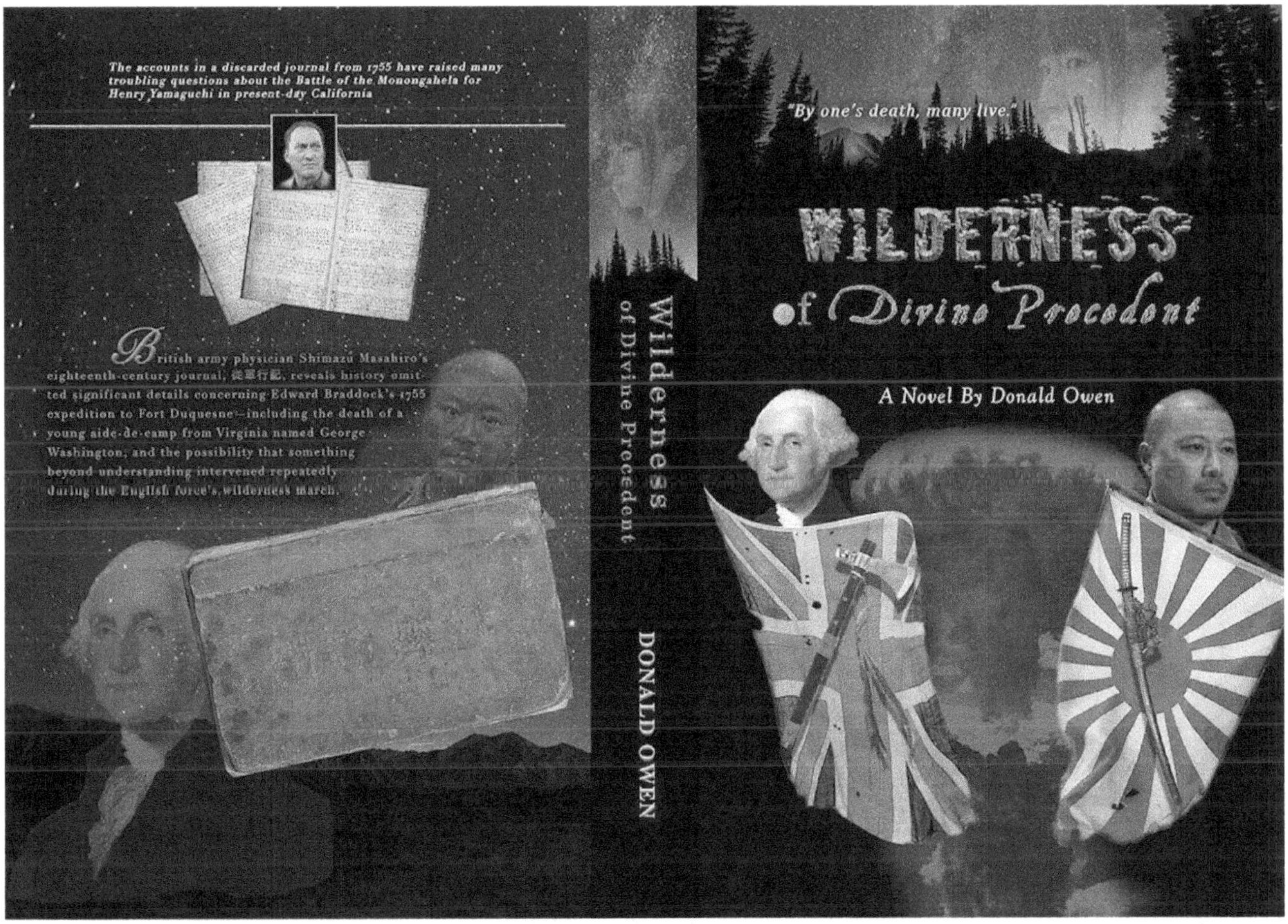

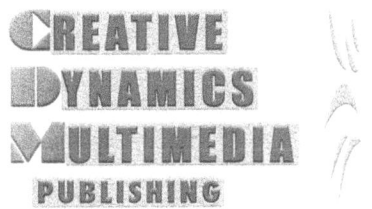

www.ingramcontent.com/pod-product-compliance
Lightning Source LLC
Chambersburg PA
CBHW081216170526
45165CB00009B/2845

9 781548 053789